IT'S TIME TO

FIX

YOURSELF

Rabia Farheen

Salman Raza Bukhari

ii | P a g e

About Authors

Rabia Farheen is an Electrical and Electronics Engineer. She was born in Pakistan's Lahore city. She is quite interested in researching the advancement of technology in all fields (Engineering, Medical, Information Technology and Education), as well as the Psychological and Social issues, Cultures and Civilizations of many regions. She enjoys exploring new places and was motivated to create wonderful and stunning Handmade and Digital Calligraphy paintings by her interest in Calligraphy and Painting. She is certified Graphic Designer, Content Writer and Digital Marketer.

Electrical Engineer **Hafiz Syed M. Salman Raza Bukhar**i is from Pakistan. His specialization is in Power System. He studies software and digital design as well. He is also interested in study of Economics and Business, technological advancements, Art and Culture. Together with Rabia he worked on IoT based Medical Robotics and many other projects of Electronics and Power System.

Dedication

Thank you Dear God Almighty for giving us the courage and everything in our life. Dedicated to our wonderful parents, families, teachers, and friends, whose unwavering support and collaboration helped us achieve this amazing feat.

"Dedicated to our beloved ones"

Acknowledgement

We are thankful to our Creator God Almighty, who giving us the courage and everything in our life. We want to thank our parents and friends for being with us and to support us in every situation. Thank you so much to encourage and guide us in every task of life. You have always stand with us and make us realized that we are not alone and there is something special in us. More essential than monetary or material rewards is achievement. More personal pleasure results from achieving the goal or job. Every achievement takes a team effort, and this task is no different. To all who may have helped with this effort, Anonymously, I would want to convey my appreciation.

Preface

A self-improvement strategy enables you to build the life you really desire for yourself. It enables you to maintain perspective on your priorities and the things that are most important to you in life so that you experience greater meaning and fulfillment. Setting priorities in your life is necessary for self-improvement. Enhancing strengths, enhancing mental health, and even mending relationships are all benefits of self-improvement.

Little actions like reading a book, trying something new, meditating, or simply getting up early are some methods to better oneself. Self-improvement is the process of actively working to better one's knowledge, status, or character. It's our constant effort to improve in all spheres of life.

About Book

In this book we are going to guide you that how to improve yourself. You will learn that how to act in panic situations, how to take decisions, how discipline be, and how to admire yourself and others. In this book there are many examples and success and failure stories which may inspire you.

Your ability to accomplish your goals is fueled by your motivation. This book will have an uplifting and upbeat effect on your life. It will give you more self-assurance and support the development of a positive view on life. Reading this book will teach you your potential strength in life.

Table of Contents

Chapter 1

Admire Yourself

Admire Yourself

If you don't appreciate what you currently have, why should more good things come your way?

People frequently forget to love themselves in today's fast-paced world when everyone is engaged in a rat race. The expression "I don't like myself" is one that you could hear individuals use frequently.

More pitiful still, many people don't even understand why they despise themselves. We may express the phrase "I don't like myself" for a variety of reasons, including fear of being rejected; lack of confidence; overanalyzing; intense anger; nervousness; lack of adjustment; and a host of other reasons. They have a profound psychological effect on us and drive us to despise who we are and the life we lead.

Be your own best buddy when life gets challenging or lonely. We often hear the saying, "We are our worst enemy," and it couldn't be more accurate. Decide to be your own best buddy instead. When the rest of the world doesn't understand you, it becomes essential to understand yourself. You become autonomous when you act as your own tour guide. Spend some time learning more about your preferences. Enjoy being alone while engaging in your favorite activities. Increase your self-discovery.

Admire and respect who you are as a person:

Almost every element of your life, including your welfare, your relationships, and the way you see and experience the world, is influenced by the relationship you have with yourself. The basis of this connection is self-worth.

When you value yourself, you are willing to devote time and effort to bettering yourself and achieving your objectives because you feel that you are worthy of respect, love, and success. There are numerous things you can do to work towards increasing your feeling of self-worth, even if it might be a long-term struggle.

Self-worth and self-value are two ideas that are frequently used in conjunction with one another. "The perception of one's own value or worth as a person" is the definition of self-worth. Self-value extends beyond believing that you are deserving or significant. Self-value, according to Stony, "is more behavioral than emotional, more about how you act toward what you value, including yourself than how you feel about yourself in comparison to others."

In order to maintain and nurture oneself, you must be willing to devote time and effort to doing so. This is what it means to have self-value. It is not selfish to value yourself by emphasizing needs and wants; rather, it is a necessary step to boosting your self-confidence and enhancing significant relationships in your life.

A key component of having a life where you feel good about yourself without any outside help or influence is believing in your value. You may comprehend and think you are deserving of love, kindness, and good things in life if you value yourself first. When you have these beliefs, it is simpler to enjoy external affirmation and appreciation when it occurs.

No amount of love, acclaim, or approval from outside sources can satisfy you if you don't appreciate yourself. Devaluing oneself, on the other hand, will make you feel as though you are not worthy of such honors. Additionally, it might also lead you to suffer more negative self-talk and encounter more self-esteem and self-image concerns.

According to a University of Michigan study, college students who place a high value on things like appearance, social acceptance, and academic stress report higher levels of stress, anger, academic problems, relationship conflicts, and drug and alcohol use, as well as signs of eating disorders. They also report higher levels of stress and other negative emotions.

The same study also discovered that adolescents who derived their sense of value from internal qualities like virtue or adherence to moral principles performed better academically and were less likely to abuse drugs or alcohol or develop eating problems.

According to a different study, those who have high self-esteem experience less emotional pain while receiving unfavorable criticism from others. The study amply demonstrates the significance of developing a strong feeling of internal self-value rather than pinning your worth and value on other people or things.

How to increase your own worth:

It takes work to increase your sense of worth, but happily, there are things you can do to support yourself.

Quit evaluating yourself against others:

Comparing yourself to others and believing that you are not doing enough or are deficient in some area of life is something that we all do. Your sense of self-worth and general mental health may suffer if you constantly compare yourself to others.

What other people are doing, thinking about you, or what they have done is irrelevant. The value you place on yourself personally is significantly more crucial to cultivate and uphold. Although it is easier said than done, you may start to concentrate on your own particular path, your objectives, and what you particularly value in life when you stop comparing yourself to others.

Establish limits:

Boundaries you set for yourself and your sense of self-worth go hand in hand. You get to decide how you want to be treated by others when you set personal limits for yourself. They provide you the power to defend yourself against unfair treatment or exploitation. It is evident that you respect yourself and want the same respect from others when you have a strong sense of self-worth and clear limits.

Setting boundaries might occasionally seem awkward because we worry that doing so would make us appear rude or self-centered. Though it can frequently result in a pattern of ignoring yourself in order to please others or accepting disrespectful or destructive conduct, you are doing yourself a disservice if you don't create clear and respected boundaries in your life.

The more people will treat you with the respect and compassion you deserve the more you are able to practice boundary establishment in your life, and those who are unable to respect those limits may not be conducive to the healthy relationships you need and desire in your life.

Refute your self-defeating thoughts:

How we perceive ourselves, other people and the environment is significantly influenced by our inner voice. Everyone occasionally engages in negative self-talk; it's normal! Being able to identify and contradict your critical self-talk is crucial. You will start to believe these thoughts and regard them as true if you allow your inner critic continues to flourish unchecked. It's crucial to first be able to recognize when negative self-talk is present in order to develop and maintain a strong sense of self-value.

Typical types of self-talk include:

- Personalizing is the act of placing responsibility on yourself for an event even though you had little to no control over it or had little or no influence. Personalization may be seen in ideas like "everyone hates me" or "it's all my fault."

- Catastrophizing is when you unquestioningly predict the worst-case scenario to occur. For instance, "I don't feel like hanging out with my friends right now, but if I skip the party, they won't like me anymore, and I'll be alone forever,"

- Filtering: filtering implies that you accentuate the negative components of a situation and overlook the positive. For example, you just finished playing a soccer game and your coach compliments your performance many times. In addition, he offers one piece of helpful critique. You can only concentrate on constructive criticism in place of embracing and appreciating the favorable comments.

- When you have polarized self-talk, you only perceive the positive or negative aspects of situations. An illustration of polarized thinking is the idea that you must be flawless or else you would fail.

Although overcoming this kind of self-talk might be challenging, there are steps you can take. You may confront your unfavorable beliefs by asking yourself some basic questions, like these:

- Does this idea have any supporting data?
- Is this belief true? Would other people consider it to be true?
- Am I making assumptions too soon?

Go to treatment:

Considering therapy as a way to improve your sense of worth may be very useful. Studies have shown that counseling is an effective way to address poor self-worth, self-esteem, and self-value. For instance, a case study looking at the effectiveness of Cognitive Behavioral Therapy (CBT) for a person with low self-esteem, depression, and anxiety revealed that after completing the therapy, the person no longer met the diagnostic criteria for any mental health disorder and displayed clinically significant improvement in their symptoms.

A therapist may assist you in discovering the underlying causes of any problems you might be having, such as concerns with self-worth and self-worth. A therapist may provide fresh insight, help you learn how to question negative self-talk, address prior trauma that can be a cause of low self-worth, and create healthy coping mechanisms.

Conclusion:

Among the finest things you can do for yourself is to have a strong feeling of your own worth. Although it might occasionally be challenging to appreciate oneself, there are constructive activities you can do to increase your feeling of self-worth. You may take steps toward a good transformation by putting some of the techniques outlined in this book into practice and realizing that you are worthy of respect, love, happiness, and success.

Chapter 2

Assertive

Being fair must be backed up by being aggressive and somewhat strong.

Introduction

It is seen as a crucial life skill that kids should learn, and recent research revealed that more than 50% of adults believe their lack of assertiveness has cost them opportunities at work. It is possible to learn how to communicate successfully by being assertive, which is a communication skill.

An individual uses assertiveness as a critical thinking strategy when they speak up to defend their opinions or in response to false information. The person who is not aggressive is shy, deceitful, self-denying, and emotionally dishonest. People who are assertive may speak out, assess material, and identify places where it is missing in content, specifics, or proof. Being assertive fosters original thought and excellent communication.

The amount of assertiveness displayed in each human group depends on current social and cultural norms. These elements may change over time and differ from one community to another. For instance, in the modern western world, problematic issues like drug misuse, rape, and the sexual exploitation of women and children are openly addressed in public, but they were not before 1940.

Assertiveness was greatly emphasized as a behavioral trait taught by numerous personal development experts, behavior therapists, and cognitive behavioral therapists in the latter part of the 20th century. Self-esteem and assertiveness are frequently related.

Women have always been seen as having trouble being forceful. However, Poor communication is the root cause of many violent altercations, according to research on violence and men's roles. Confrontations grow as a result of poor communication.

When confronted with hostile communication from men and women in their life, many men feel helpless; In contrast, many men might become frustrated and angry when others act passively in certain circumstances. As a result, if males want to actively reduce violence in their lives, assertiveness can be a useful technique. Lifestyles, as well as a means of promoting longer, happier lives.

According to sociologists and mental health experts, assertiveness is typically seen in specific situations. In other words, assertiveness is not a personality attribute that holds true in every circumstance. Depending on whether they are feeling confident or aggressive, different people will behave in different ways.

They are engaged in a job, social, intellectual, leisure, or romantic connection. As a result, one objective of assertiveness training is to increase the number of contexts in which a person is able to communicate firmly.

Non-Assertiveness

A non-assertive person is one who frequently falls victim to unfair treatment, feels powerless, accepts responsibility for everyone else's issues, agrees to unreasonable demands and careless requests, and lets other people make decisions for them. He or she is essentially saying, "I'm not OK."

The non-assertive individual is timid, indirect, self-denying, and emotionally dishonest. He or she is distressed, indignant, and maybe hurt by what they did.

Nonaggression Body Language

• Looking down, aside, or without making eye contact

• Moving the weight from one foot to the other while swaying.

• Whining and a speech impediment.

Assertiveness

A person who is assertive act in his or her own best interests defends themselves, communicate their emotions honestly, manage their own affairs in social situations, and make decisions for themselves. An assertive individual is emotionally honest, straightforward, self-enhancing, and vocal. Their core message is "I'm OK and you're OK." Both during acting and afterward, he or she feels assured and respectable.

Confident Body Language:

• Make eye contact with the individuals you are speaking to while standing upright, stable, and facing them directly.

• Speak clearly and steadily, loud enough so that the persons you are speaking to can hear you.

• Speak clearly, confidently, without hesitating, and with assurance.

Aggressiveness

Someone who is aggressive damages others, intimidates others, uses power to win, manipulates the environment to his or her advantage, and makes decisions for others. An aggressive person is inappropriately talkative, emotionally open, forthright, and self-enhancing at the expense of another. They declare, "You're not OK." When acting aggressively, a person feels righteous, superior, and demeaning, and they may feel bad later.

Violent body language:

• Forward slanting with blazing eyes.

• Slightly pointing your finger in the direction of the listener.

• Yelling.

· Squeezing fists together.

• Wagging the head and placing hands on hips.

Keep in mind that assertiveness is a function of both what you say and how you say it.

To Make Communication Process Better:

• Reflecting back to the other person both words and feelings while actively listening expressed by the individual.

• Defining your position: expressing your ideas and emotions around the predicament.

• Investigating different options, generating ideas, and weighing the advantages and disadvantages; evaluating potential answers.

Requesting Simple Things:

• You have the right to express your desires to other people.

• When you don't ask for what you want, you minimize your own significance.

• Directly asking for what you want is the greatest approach to acquiring it.

• It's possible that indirect requests won't be understood.

• When you present forceful body language, your request is more likely to be understood.

Requests Rejected:

• You are entitled to refuse!

• When you say yes when you actually mean no, you minimize your own significance.

• Refusing a request does not mean that you are rejecting the individual making it.

• It's crucial to be straightforward, succinct, and to the point when expressing rejection.

• Avoid being persuaded to change your mind if you truly mean to say no by appealing, begging, cajoling, praising, or several ways to manipulate.

• You may provide justifications for your refusal, but don't go overboard with them.

• A brief apology is sufficient; lengthy excuses may be disrespectful.

• Display a confident demeanor.

• Learning how to say no is a talent.

Saying no without feeling bad about it may become a habit that greatly promotes progress.

Effective "No" Expressions:

• The four guiding criteria for writing responses are succinctness, clarity, firmness, and honesty.

• Use the word "NO" at the beginning of your response to avoid any ambiguity.

• Keep your response succinct and direct.

• Don't go into much detail.

• Be direct, forthright, and firm.

• Avoid using "I'm sorry, but..."

Learning the Art of Saying "No"

• Consider if the request is reasonable.

"Hedging, doubting, feeling backed into a corner, and

Your body's tension or anxiousness are all indicators that you need to say no or desire to say no.

Additional details before making a decision.

• State that you have the right to request further details and clarity before responding.

• Say NO firmly and calmly after considering the request and deciding that you do not wish to comply.

• Practice saying NO without apologizing.

Consider Your Claims

• Actively reflecting the other person's words and thoughts back to them while listening to them expressed by the individual.

• Defining your position: expressing your ideas and emotions around the predicament.

• Investigating different options, generating ideas, and weighing the advantages and disadvantages; rating the potential answers.

Confident Techniques

1. Broken Record - Be persistent and keep expressing what you want while being calm and collected. Maintain your focus.

2. Learn to pay attention to other people and follow up on any free information they provide about themselves. You have conversation starters thanks to this free knowledge.

3. Self-Disclosure — clearly state what you know about yourself, including your thoughts, feelings, and responses to what the other person says. This reveals information about you to the other individual.

4. Fogging: Handling criticism is an aggressive coping technique. Don't dispute any criticism and refrain from coming back with your own.

• Agree with the truth - Identify a point in the critique that is accurate and support it.

Accept the probabilities - Accept any conceivable truth in the negative assertion.

• In principle concur - concur with the universal truth in a logical statement like "That makes sense."

• Bad Assertion - Making a point of acknowledging the negative aspects of oneself. Overcoming your mistakes.

• Viable Compromise - Offer a workable compromise when your self-respect is not in jeopardy.

Conflict Resolution Technique

• The situation's facts are described by both sides.

• Both sides explain how they are feeling about the circumstance and demonstrate empathy for one another.

• Both parties agree on the behavior changes they would want to see or are willing to accept.

• Take into account the outcomes. What will occur as a result of the altered behavior? Although compromise could be required, it might also be impossible. If you require further help, continue with counseling.

Individual Bill of Rights

1. The first is the right to respect.

2. The freedom to feel and voice your own thoughts and ideas.

3. The entitlement to respect and consideration.

4. The freedom to decide what matters most.

5. The freedom to refuse without feeling bad.

6. The privilege of receiving what you pay for.

7. The freedom to commit errors.

8. The freedom to decide not to make a statement

Conclusions

The quality of assertiveness is the capacity to speak up for yourself and your rights while also respecting those of others. As a result, for a romantic relationship to succeed and be healthy, it is essential for both parties to preserve their sense of self.

All aspiring leaders must gain the ability to communicate assertively. It enables you to relate with others more authentically, speak with greater assurance, and cope with challenging circumstances with ease.

You may be more satisfied at work by being assertive in order to get what you want and need. You may also advance professionally and acquire the respect of your peers. Receive individualized coaching from Better Up to learn how to be aggressive.

Chapter

3

Decision Making Skills

The best course of action is always to do what is right, and the next best course of action is always to do what is wrong.

Introduction

Decision-making abilities may make a difference in our ability to make a decision that enhances our company, our future, etc. The capacity for decision-making is always a leadership quality that demonstrates our capacity for critical thinking to advance our objectives. We can develop our organizational culture by building great relationships with all of the employees thanks to our ability to act quickly.

These abilities demonstrate our ability to make decisions when faced with two or more options. Once we have analyzed all the facts at our disposal and have spoken with the pertinent parties engaged in the matter, we may make choices. As a result, it's critical to recognize the procedures that guide our decision-making on behalf of the business and to make a concerted effort to detect biases that may potentially have an impact.

The Following is a List of Some Decision-Making Abilities

- **Dilemma Solving**

Leaders use their capacity for problem-solving to reach important corporate choices. In order to properly analyze the many diverse factors, we must take into account many points of view. We must also keep our emotions apart from the talks we conduct with others who will have an impact on our decision-making. In order to effectively solve problems, we must be able to make judgments swiftly and efficiently. To match the facts with the problem we are addressing, we must conduct extensive study and pay special attention to every detail.

- **Command**

It is described as the process of bringing together a number of personnel inside the business and effective leadership that can forge a consensus over a certain course of action. In that situation, leadership is working with the group to assess the situation at hand and inspire them to pursue the chosen course of action. In order to get to know our coworkers and have them feel comfortable speaking openly around us, we should always make sure that we invest the time necessary to develop solid relationships with them. The more involved and approachable we are, the more likely it is that we will get along with the team and make decisions that will benefit us in the long run.

- **Justification**

One of the key competencies required to fully understand the decision we are making will be this one. Every option that we contemplate acting on should have its benefits and drawbacks carefully considered. It is always preferable to have an open mind and maintain your sense of reality while making plans for the future. To support a decision on whom we are making it, we should take into account all pertinent and readily available evidence. We should constantly seek to maintain our commitment to the objectives we are attempting to attain and keep our thinking in line with the individuals we trust.

- **Perception**

Simply choosing to believe our instincts is intuition. Instincts are a result of the previous events we have lived through and the guiding principles that guide us every day. Our decision-making is influenced by our cumulative experiences and the lessons we have learnt from our intuition. To determine if a choice is reasoned and practicable, we must always connect our intuition with the possible courses of action.

- **Collaboration**

At some point, we should always work together with our teammates to reach a wise choice. The finest strategy to collaborate with the customer and enhance the outcomes of their marketing campaign from the previous quarter may require us to coordinate with our marketing manager. To assist the customer to enhance their campaign, we always utilize logic to deconstruct the alternatives so that a status report may provide us with pertinent information. Then, we may evaluate the potential KPIs that will be used to gauge its success moving forward. Overall, our capacity for teamwork affects the outcomes we achieve and the number of individuals whose lives are impacted by the choices our team makes.

- **Emotional Awareness**

Due to our increased emotional awareness and ability to convey our feelings in ways that inspire action. Our motivation for a certain cause or objective should always have to begin with our emotions as the foundation. The manner in which we examine the relevant evidence will always determine how well-informed we are when coming to a choice.

- **Innovation**

Our logical and emotional thinking is combined with creativity to provide an original answer. In order to share ideas and develop both short-term and long-term solutions, the company has to have dependable personnel. To make sure that everyone's viewpoint is heard, we may always utilize our own creativity to shape the discussions we have with the staff during meetings and the time allotted. As a result, we can have weekly brainstorming sessions to foster employee creativity and provide valuable ideas.

- **Manipulation of Time**

Decisions must always be made fast, thus we should specify how much time we have to decide. While we must work within the constraints of our circumstances, time management gives us the framework we need to come to a choice. If we have a week or a day to make a decision, we may take our time considering all of the options, including potential courses of action and suggested solutions.

- **Institution**

In coming to a choice, the organization is crucial. This ability should be used to determine the outcomes we seek and whether they are of the utmost importance. The goal of surveys regarding a product is to get input from the target market and determine if the current user persona is being used to sell the campaign.

- **Mental bias**

The decision-making process can be disrupted and distorted by cognitive bias or inherent prejudice. Confirmation, anchoring, the halo effect, and overconfidence are some of the most prevalent biases.

- **Revelation**

When a decision is made to seek out data that supports a previously held idea while rejecting evidence that supports other hypotheses, this is referred to as confirmation.

- **Establishing**

This is when a person bases too many decisions on a single piece of knowledge or experience.

- **The Halo Impact**

It is the general opinion of the business, particular brand, or product that directly affects the emotions and ideas of the person.

- **Confirmation bias.**

When someone exaggerates how trustworthy our judgments are, this happens.

- **Cooperation**

One individual cannot always make decisions. To make the optimal option, which may occasionally be a collective decision, we must constantly have strong teamwork skills. Getting additional feedback from friends or coworkers who can help us brainstorm the ideal solution is helpful even when we are ready to make a choice on our own. When both of us must participate in a collective decision and when we are the one who must make the choice, collaboration is our buddy.

- **Logical Thinking**

The ability that is essential for the middle stages of the decision-making process is logical thinking. We are able to thoroughly assess and examine the data, choices, and decisions that go into our collective decision. This ability is more directly tied to thinking, the part of decision-making that is supported by data and logic rather than feelings.

To Enhance the Capacity for Making Decisions

We may utilize the following ideas to hone our decision-making abilities:

- **Describe the Circumstance**

Any employee in the company is expected to recognize issues. Depending on the severity, we should always report to the department manager or human resources. It's also possible to let the executive team know that it's connected to the long-term objectives they've established. Before proceeding with alerting the rest of the company, schedule a meeting with all stakeholders concerned.

- **Make a Note of Probable Remedies or Steps**

Record and maintain a list of all potential solutions to the situation at hand. They will be listed in front of our team at a meeting so they may take part in the discussion. In order for them to retain a record of it, it should also be provided by email. All the team members are given a list of prospective actions to do once all the options have been presented in order to carry out the decision that has been reached.

- **Listing Each Option's Benefits and Drawbacks.**

To ensure that choices can go to the decision-making stage, we should thoroughly analyze the advantages and disadvantages. To determine whether it aligns with our objectives and KPIs that evaluate our performance, we should think about taking our time and carefully weighing the benefits and drawbacks.

- **Selecting the Choices We Wish to Make and Evaluating the Outcomes**

Consider the choices we make as having both immediate and long-term effects. The good news is that we always gain knowledge from the choices we make, therefore we should monitor the decision's performance to ensure that the results match up with all of the advantages and disadvantages we have identified.

Conclusion:

Our capacity for decision-making may affect our capacity to make choices that benefit our business, our future, etc. Leaders utilize their ability to solve problems to arrive at crucial business decisions. It is more probable that we will get along with the team and make judgments that will be advantageous to us in the long term if we are more engaged and approachable. Justification will be one of the major skills needed to comprehend the decision we are making completely. Our cumulative experiences and the lessons we've learned from our intuition have an impact on our decision-making. We should constantly state how much time we have to decide since decisions must be made quickly. Think of the decisions we make as having both short-term and long-term consequences.

Chapter

4

Positive Strength

*It might occasionally seem like a
burden, but that is not what makes
you unique. It's also frequently what
distinguishes you as a person.*

Every person is unique, and depending on our personalities, we all behave differently. Finding your strengths and getting to know yourself are vital. You may capitalize on your abilities and use them to advance in both your personal and professional lives.

However, this does not imply that these flaws will be your undoing. There is need for improvement in these areas. It is not something you lack; rather, it is something you must grow and develop. Finding Your

Strengths is the first step in using your strengths and strengthening your deficiencies.

Discovering Your Abilities

One of your greatest personal strengths would be something you do extremely naturally. Think about what comes easily to you for a while; it may be anything. You could have little trouble striking up discussions with strangers or be very adept at finding solutions in a tent atmosphere. Knowing your flaws is just as crucial as identifying your strengths.

Why Do You Find Your Strengths?

You may better understand yourself and how you function by being aware of your strengths and shortcomings. Finding Your Strengths If you were considering career alternatives, you might be able to focus on a certain position based on the skills you are confident in having. Additionally, understanding your strengths empowers you to set higher standards for yourself and accomplish more. Understanding your shortcomings also helps you identify any potential obstacles in your path. So that your deficiencies don't limit you, you may then focus on these areas.

Concentrate on Identifying Your Weaknesses or Strengths

- Focusing on discovering your strengths is preferable. You don't need to spend as much time honing those particular areas because they are the things you're already strong at. In order to find your strengths, you must look for chances and issues. Concentrating on your faults, seeing your strengths as issues rather than triumphs. It also lowers your self-confidence, excitement, and general performance to concentrate on your areas of weakness. But improving your areas of weakness is just as crucial for your personal development. If you can get better at something you weren't really strong at, even little, it may make a significant difference in how well you do overall. Avoid attempting to eliminate or cure your deficiencies; this is ineffective. Find strategies to get around your shortcomings so they don't get in the way of your goals or hamper you. Gaining an understanding of your strengths and flaws is equally vital. Anyone's personal growth and development depend on it. If you are aware of your own potential and what you are capable of, there are many things you can do.

Finding Your Strengths Has These Five Advantages

- **You get to save time:**

Knowing when you did a good job as a parent will not only save you time, but it will also prevent you from having to teach us again. Not that you were attempting to study or look into different employment opportunities, but being aware of the qualities and skills you possess will enable you to make immediate decision-making.

- **Enables you to expand even more:**

Knowing your strengths and areas of excellence can enable you to expand your horizons and achieve new heights. If you merely understand Finding Your Strengths, you can do so much more than you ever imagined.

- **Increase your confidence:**

Whatever they may be, identifying your strong areas can help you feel more confident. Even if they are

minor talents, they will boost your confidence, which will enable you to do more.

- **Increases your happiness:**

When you were discovering your strengths, you felt more confident in yourself and that you could accomplish anything. Anyone will be pleased knowing they have a skill set that will provide them an advantage.

- **You can serve as an example and a mentor to others:**

You may utilize your own talents to inspire or direct others once you've taken the effort to identify them. You may set a good example for other people, and your supervisor will appreciate it.

What you receive from PDP FYNS is Finding Your Strengths

You stand for fundamental character attributes. Your unique strengths are encoded in your traits. Making use of your strengths leads to success and pleasure. Your decision-making process and rationale. How you think through and make choices. Your dynamism patterns how do you go about completing chores or achieving your goals? These are all factors in "Finding Your Strengths."

Finding Your Strengths PDPFYNS

There is a three-step approach at PDPFYNS to assist you in discovering your strengths. Taking the Pros can survey is the first step. The survey takes between 5 and 10 minutes to complete, after which you receive a copy of your customized Finding Your Strengths report in your mailbox and a link to access it on your device. Experience your strengths as the next step. Reviewing your Finding Your Strengths report is enjoyable. Gain a comprehensive grasp of your strengths to enable you to lead a meaningful life. Learn and develop, you are now prepared to go on the road of living from your strength in order to achieve greater levels of fulfilment. You may follow the procedure with the help of sources. Along with other educational opportunities, you may also share the Finding Your Strengths report with one another.

Finding Your Strengths PDPFYNS

There is a three-step approach at PDPFYNS to assist you in discovering your strengths. Taking the Pros can survey is the first step. The survey takes between 5 and 10 minutes to complete, after which you receive a copy of your customized Finding Your Strengths report in your mailbox and a link to access it on your device. Experience your strengths as the next step. Reviewing your Finding Your Strengths report is enjoyable. Gain a comprehensive grasp of your strengths to enable you to lead a meaningful life. Learn and develop. You are now prepared to go on the road of living from your strength in order to achieve greater levels of fulfilment. You may follow the procedure with the help of sources.

Conclusion:

Every individual is different, and our personalities influence how each of us behaves. Knowing yourself and identifying your abilities are essential. Something you do very naturally would be one of your biggest personal talents. Knowing your talents and weaknesses may help you get a better understanding of who you are and how you work. You need to explore for opportunities and problems in order to identify your skills. Focusing on your shortcomings and viewing your accomplishments as challenges rather than victories. Knowing when you were a good parent can help you save time and spare you from having to teach us again. In order to experience greater levels of fulfillment, you are now ready to go on the path of living from your strength.

Chapter

5

Willingness to Take a Chance

Taking a risk is the only way we have to have a chance of realizing our ambitions, and most individuals who are plagued by negative self-talk do not think the risk is worthwhile.

Where do you wish you had been a bit braver, more confident in yourself, and less careful in the risks you made when you reflect on your work and life to date?

What comes to mind? When I talk to people in their forties and beyond, many of them say that they would have taken more chances, settled less, and spoken up more frequently if they could go back in time. In other words, they regretted not being bolder in their risk-taking. Maybe you can relate.

Even when we are aware of what we want to achieve, we frequently fail to take action. Why? We are inherently risk-averse and wary of exposing our vulnerability, even when the status quo is unfulfilling, it might appear to be a simpler, kinder, less frightening choice. In fact, developments in brain imaging technology now allow us to confirm that humans are hardwired to be risk adverse. To put it another way, we prefer over maintain the status quo, keep our mouths shut, and keep our heads down to making changes, taking risks, or having what I refer to as "courageous conversations."

We have an intrinsic propensity to misunderstand four key components in assessing risk when deciding whether to follow a course of action that might leave us exposed to failure or some other type of loss (of reputation, money, social status, pride, etc.).

- We exaggerate the likelihood that things will go wrong. Prospective losses frequently loom bigger when evaluating risk than potential profits, as Daniel Kahneman noted in Thinking, Fast and Slow. That is, rather than concentrating on what may go well, we frequently think about what might go wrong—what we might forfeit or lose. We tend to overestimate the chance of what we focus on since our imaginations tend to exaggerate what we focus on. The odds of something turning out well are frequently much higher than we anticipate, while the danger of it not working out is frequently much lower.

- We overestimate the possibility that something will go wrong. When assessing risk, possible losses usually overshadow potential gains, as Daniel Kahneman discovered in Thinking, Fast and Slow. In other words, rather of focusing on what may go right, what we might sacrifice or lose, we typically consider what might go wrong. Since our imaginations tend to exaggerate what we focus on, we tend to overestimate the likelihood of what we focus on. While the likelihood of anything going wrong is typically lot lower than we think, the likelihood of it working out is frequently considerably higher.

- We underestimate our capacity to deal with risk's effects. This complements the previous but focuses more on our overall competence. I detest to say it, but women are the worst offenders when it comes to undervaluing their skills and succumbing to self-doubt. Too frequently, we allow our doubts about our abilities to achieve to overcome us. As a result, we frequently shy away from accepting new challenges (or aggressively chasing new possibilities) because we lack enough confidence in our capacity to successfully navigate the difficulties they provide. Speaking at an Ernst & Young event for women in leadership, managing partner Lynn Kraus told me how she first turned down multiple offers to take on senior leadership positions before deciding to accept one. She had declined each offer because she didn't believe she could be successful in the role. Lynn realized she had been seriously underestimating herself when she looked back, now that she had been in the position for a while. She was fortunate in that people who spotted her potential weren't quick to give up on her. However, how frequently do we misjudge our own ability to take on risks, such as assuming a larger responsibility or pursuing a challenging objective? In my opinion, that happens far too frequently.

- We minimize or downplay the price of inactivity and maintaining the status quo. In a previous piece titled The Parmenides Fallacy, I discussed this. Do

You Disregard the Price of Inaction? We convince ourselves that things aren't as awful as they seem in the hopes that things will eventually "figure themselves out" and become better. We make up justifications for why maintaining the status quo is a viable choice and why it is "logical" to play it safe and avoid taking unnecessary risks. In truth, when we ignore problems in our relationships and lives, they tend to get bigger, not less, and things that aren't going well for us right now only seem to get worse over time, not better.

These four different human tendencies acting in concert help to explain why so many supposedly intelligent people live in such a constrained range of their potential, feel unfulfilled in their careers, get stuck in their relationships, and lead lives they would never have chosen, much less aspired to.

How then can we get above this inclination to keep it safe and decide which chances are worth taking? Start by posing these three questions to yourself:

1. How would I respond if I had greater courage?

2. How much would my inaction cost me in a year if I don't take any action?

3. Where is my fear of failing making me underestimate myself, exaggerate the extent of the danger, and refrain from taking chances that would benefit me (my business, etc.)?

Whatever responses cross your thoughts, pay attention! They are guiding you in the direction of a more promising future that you can only achieve by deciding to behave braver, more determined, and more boldly. Are there any potential risks? Of course! However, keep in mind that you are hardwired to exaggerate their size and underestimate your capacity to handle them. You are capable of more than you realize, as Lao Tsu stated more than 2,000 years ago. Fear regret more than failure because, as history has demonstrated, we falter from timidity more often than from over daring.

Conclusions:

We overestimate the possibility that anything will go wrong. We underestimate our ability to manage the repercussions of risk. This adds to the first while putting a stronger emphasis on our general competency. While the probability of something going wrong is often far lower than we believe, the probability of it succeeding is frequently much higher. Things that aren't going well for us right now really appear to become worse over time, not better, and when we overlook difficulties in our relationships and lives, they tend to get greater, not less. You are programmed to overestimate their magnitude and underestimate your ability to handle them, so keep that in mind.

Chapter
6

Develop Self-Compassion

Just being nice to ourselves as we would be good to others is self-compassion.

Giving attention to the physical, spiritual, and emotional needs of others, including ourselves, is the attitude that serves as the foundation for all other depression-relieving techniques. Everything else gets much simpler if we can learn to love and support ourselves through our problems.

Have you ever become irate with yourself? Accused of doing something you regret, and then slightly beat yourself up internally for it?

Perhaps after being harsh with someone, you were even worse on yourself? It's simple to be hard on oneself; we do it a lot more often than we know. But what if a better option existed? Self-compassion is a skill that we may develop through forgiving ourselves, accepting our apparent imperfections, and being kind to ourselves. While making it a habit that stays is frequently much difficult than it seems, we may learn the proper methods.

Some of these approaches may be helpful if you ever criticize or criticize yourself without cause. While some may not be your cup of tea, others may strike a chord and prove useful at unexpected times. Continue reading for advice and activities on how to practice self-compassion, then let us know what works for you. We may be kind to ourselves by having self-compassion, and it is a notion that can be experimentally measured. It is made up of three distinct constructs: self-kindness, common humanity, and mindfulness. Associate

Professor Dr. Kristin Neff operationalized this concept and brought it to the literature on positive psychology. When circumstances are less than ideal, being able to relate to yourself in a way that is forgiving, accepting, and loving is a sign of self-compassion. How do we demonstrate self-compassion? We are aware that it is different from self-esteem and that it is akin to (though less lasting than) self-love.

Self-Kindness:

Self-kindness entails being understanding and nice to oneself when we make mistakes or experience pain. When we already experience suffering, we may identify the harmful effects of self-judgment and treat ourselves with kindness and compassion rather than being harsh or judgmental of ourselves. In other words, practicing self-kindness entails accepting our value regardless of whether we fall short of our own standards through our actions or even simply our thoughts.

Following are a few instances taken from the Self-Compassion Scale (SCS):

- Extending to yourself the compassion and care you require through trying times.

- Making an effort to comprehend and be patient with your own apparent personality defects.
- Being understanding of your own flaws.

Typical Humanity:

Positive psychology literature frequently uses the phrase "becoming part of something greater," and it has long been maintained that people naturally seek for relationships. To consider our own unique experiences as part of the larger human experience, as opposed to perceiving ourselves as isolated or distinct from others, is to have common humanity.

We are not flawless, but we demonstrate self-compassion when we are lenient with ourselves for having limits. Accepting and forgiving ourselves for our imperfections is part of this. Realizing that we're not the only ones who make mistakes or experience pain is another aspect of shared humanity; rather than retreating or isolating ourselves, we acknowledge that other people experience these things occasionally.

More specific behaviors, in accordance with the SCS, might include:

- Believing that your flaws are normal elements of being human.

- Assuming that your struggles are "part of life that everyone experiences."

- Recognizing when you're feeling inadequate that other people go through the same thing.

Mindfulness

According to self-compassion theory, mindfulness is the antithesis of avoidance or over-identification since it involves naming and admitting our own thoughts as opposed to responding to them.

Self-compassion allows us to recognize our own negative feelings and ideas without exaggerating their importance by ruminating. Instead, we strike a happy medium between the extremes of this over-identification and full avoidance of unpleasant feelings and events. These are some actions that example SCS items for mindfulness translate into:

- Attempting to maintain emotional equilibrium when confronted with distress.

- Keeping our stance when we struggle with topics that are significant to us.
- Accepting our feelings of sadness with openness and inquiry.

Practice Self-Compassion:

The goal is to maintain (or strive for) a balance between these three theoretical spectra:

- Self-kindness to self-judgment throughout the process.
- Isolation from Common Humanity.
- With mindfulness serving as the ideal middle ground between avoidance and over identification.

The words empathy, compassion, forgiveness, caring, tenderness, and different synonyms for acceptance and non-judgment are also emerging as important concepts, many of which you may already be extremely acquainted with. However, since so much of our mental activity is entrenched or automatic, it might first need some conscious effort to begin engaging in self-compassion.

How to Begin

Dr. Kristin Neff herself observes that beginning might frequently need a significant shift in perspective due to our ingrained responses to pain and bad emotions (Neff, 2019). Additionally, it requires work because we're truly attempting to adopt new strategies rather than elicit happy feelings:

"Self-compassion is a practice of goodwill, not good feelings... With self-compassion we mindfully accept that the moment is painful, and embrace ourselves with kindness and care in response, remembering that imperfection is part of the shared human experience."

(Neff, 2019)

In light of this, we'll discuss some methods and advice for putting this goodness into action before providing you with some tools, affirmations, and strategies to support you on your journey.

Self-Compassion Training Techniques:

Online resources abound with targeted activities that might help you cultivate self-compassion in a way that works for you. The majority of them follow the same general methodology, and we'll go into more detail about some of these in our Resources section.

Be kind to yourself like you would a friend:

Consider how you would treat people you care about as a good place to start. Therefore, even while we can't always make other people's grief go away, we can acknowledge it exists and offer assistance to enable them to go through it and develop. With regard to: Allow yourself to make errors. Self-kindness and general humanity draw on two distinct but connected concepts: "We're human. However, if everyone else is, it's alright since. We can let ourselves off the hook when we might do the same for others by not taking our ideas, feelings, and behaviors to be who we are. You won't likely conclude a buddy is a nasty person right away if they become unresponsive to your phone call because they were being lazy. One approach to embrace your shortcomings and remember you're not alone in being flawed is to sometimes give yourself permission to be human.

Treating oneself well is a good rule of thumb. This advice, which is closely connected to the last one, is about having compassion and understanding for oneself. You could give a buddy a physical pat on the back or hold their hand if you see that they are feeling depressed, hurt, or unhappy. These, according to Neff, are techniques for activating our own "caregiving system" and releasing oxytocin, a hormone with advantageous cardiovascular benefits. Even if we are first resistant, these actions, along with gentle, forgiving words (like calling oneself "darling" or "sweetheart"), can help us sense self-kindness. Obviously, if it feels too strange, try to restrain yourself from using too many cutesy phrases.

Conclusions

All other depression-relieving methods are built on the attitude of attending to the bodily, spiritual, and emotional needs of others, as well as our own. Being forgiving and compassionate to oneself when we make errors or endure pain is a component of self-kindness. When we are already experiencing sorrow, we may be able to see the negative impacts of self-judgment and choose to be kind and compassionate toward ourselves as opposed to being harsh or critical of ourselves. Having shared humanity is seeing our own experiences as being a part of the wider human experience rather than seeing ourselves as separate or unique from others. Self-compassion enables us to acknowledge our own unfavorable thoughts and feelings without overemphasizing them via rumination.

Chapter

7

Increasing Self-Awareness

Not never falling but rising every time we do is what makes life most glorious.

Other methods involve increasing our level of self-awareness and engaging our inner dialogue. Being conscious of our internal narratives is a good place to start for altering our self-talk as opposed to "beating ourselves up for beating ourselves up."

- Make use of "Releasing Statements." Perhaps you've never been a big believer in affirmations. You could feel uncomfortable with them or think your Inner Critic isn't quite 'reachable' via them. If so, you might want to attempt what is known as "releasing assertions" informally. These draw on the idea of detached non-judgment found in mindfulness and are closely linked to, if not the same as, mini-exercises in self-forgiveness. Try flipping the idea around and "releasing" yourself from the emotion when you notice yourself having a negative thought, such as "I'm such a bad person for becoming upset." Try "It's alright that I felt upset" instead.

- Try accepting yourself. This entails accepting both your character strengths and your perceived areas of weakness in yourself. Self-compassion is not exaggerating our flaws as a statement about who we are; rather, thoughts and feelings are actions and moods.

- Engage in mindfulness. According to Harvard, engaging in mindfulness exercises might help us to ground ourselves in the present. Not only is mindfulness one of the fundamental elements of self-compassion, but many practices like yoga and deep breathing can be done anywhere, at any time.

- Try not to be too hasty to judge oneself. DiPirro also advises against supposing that you will act in a particular manner. It's simple to make assumptions like, "I become extremely cranky and antisocial on flights," which occasionally rules out the potential that you'll behave differently. This is only a future-oriented technique to give oneself the benefit of the doubt and is yet another instance of treating yourself as you would treat others.

Gaining Prospective:

There's no denying that we currently face significant problems on all fronts—personally, nationally, and internationally. Sometimes it might all feel too much, especially if we incessantly monitor or listen to the news. This harmful energy can influence us deeply, harming our general wellbeing. Losing perspective is incredibly simple to do.

Each of us has a different strategy for getting through trying situations. Some people use relaxation techniques, while others resort to physical activity, interests, friends, family, and therapists. We all require reminders to do this, though, as well as a fresh viewpoint on the situation.

Even though we may feel helpless and incapable of handling our problems, we do have some control over our feelings and responses. Although many individuals are relying on their own resources and what has previously worked for them, our present circumstance is extremely unique, so learning new coping mechanisms may be beneficial during these times.

For me personally, my style of dealing with challenges—which has always been via writing—emerges. Many of our habits and ways of being were nurtured during infancy. My mother gave me a diary and I am grateful for her.

Therapy wasn't as popular back then as it is today, so individuals either buried their feelings or confided in close friends or family. I was a shy 10-year-old and needed a way to express my emotions because my mother was going through her own loss.

Manage Your Thoughts

— *"The energy of the mind is the essence of life."* — Aristotle

We have the ability to control our thoughts by maintaining a sense of emotional balance and well-being. Being present in the moment requires a lot of thought on the present. We tend to live in the future or dwell on the past too much when we are afraid. Proper breathing exercises can support our practice of mindfulness.

"By being able to control your breathing, by harnessing this incredibly powerful life force, you can control the way you feel. You can find calm in moments of stress. You can easily cope with almost any pressure." writes Paul Wilson in his book Instant Calm.

Try using the 4/7/8 breathing method, which is taking a breath in for four counts, holding it for seven, and then expelling for eight. It truly does work. The mind, body, and spirit are all given a lot of vitality by this practice. When we are in the moment and in control of our thoughts, we are self-aware.

Encourage Kindness

"Great acts are made up of small deeds." —Lao Tzu

According to studies, being nice to others can improve one's psychological wellbeing and boost one's immune system. Being compassionate also deflects attention from our own pressing issues.

People need to feel linked to one another since they are social creatures. Acts of kindness during these trying times can take many forms, from giving to or helping at a local food bank to sending an email to someone who has been lonely and isolated. One of the nicest things we can do when we're anxious or sad is to help someone else.

Think Of All Experiences As Just That Experiences

"It is important to expect nothing, to take every experience, including the negatives ones, as merely steps on the path, and to proceed." —Ram Dass

Consider the lessons you learned through the quarantine. Did you come to understand what matters most to you in life as a result? Did it clarify what you should be thankful for? Many people have learned to examine within thanks to this time spent by themselves, something they may not have had the opportunity to do in the past.

Consider the lessons you learned through the quarantine. Did you come to understand what matters most to you in life as a result? Did it clarify what you should be thankful for? Many people have learned to examine within thanks to this time spent by themselves, something they may not have had the opportunity to do in the past.

So many of us want to escape unpleasant circumstances in order to save ourselves the suffering and anguish they bring. Try to make room for experiences that are happy, sad, joyful, or painful. Pray, meditate, or do anything else you need to do to find consolation in the suffering.

"Everything can be taken from a man, but one thing: the last of human freedoms—to choose one's attitude in any given set of circumstances, to choose one's own way." remarked Austrian psychiatrist and Holocaust survivor Viktor Frankl. It's more important how you handled the situation and how it changed who you are than the experience itself.

Be Innovative

"Great art is the outward expression of an inner life in the artist, and this inner life will result in his personal vision of the world." *—Edward Hopper*

You may express yourself more freely when you're creative. Additionally, it effectively lessens anxiousness. Before the epidemic, you might not have had the opportunity to do anything creative, but you might have thought about doing something creative at some point—painting, knitting, making music, or writing, for instance. A wonderful moment to consider what genuinely speaks to you is right now.

This will not only improve your mood and give you a sense of purpose, but it will also make you feel proud and accomplished. Additionally, you can have a chance to meet people who take part in similar activities.

Laugh

"Laughter is the sun that drives winter from the human face." —Victor Hugo

It's a well-known proverb that "laughter is the best medicine." Even though it might be challenging to laugh at times since life can be so challenging, there is always something to find humorous. Laughter is a feel-good exercise. For funny options, turn on the TV or go online. Check out some satirical books or books written by humorists if you enjoy reading.

An excellent stress reducer is laughter. The Mayo Clinic claims that it can excite your organs since it raises the endorphins your brain releases while also enhancing your heart, lungs, and muscles and improving your oxygen intake. By generating neuropeptides that aid in the battle against stress and possibly fatal illnesses, it can also strengthen your immune system.

Perhaps at this moment it would be wise to imagine oneself in space, looking down on Earth. Although the situation here seems grave, it may all be seen as rather small in light of what is going on in the cosmos. Having this vantage point can aid us with coping mechanisms for daily life.

Conclusions

. It is undeniable that we are now experiencing serious issues on all fronts, including locally, nationally, and globally. It may all seem a little overwhelming at times, especially if we are always watching or listening to the news. Despite the fact that we can feel powerless and incapable of solving our problems, we do have some influence over how we feel and act. For me personally, my preferred method of handling difficulties has always been via writing. People either repressed their feelings or confided in close friends or family back then because therapy wasn't as common as it is today. By preserving a feeling of emotional equilibrium and wellbeing, we have the capacity to manage our thoughts. It takes much thought to be fully in the present.

Studies show that being kind to others can enhance psychological health and strengthen the immune system. Compassion often draws attention away from our own urgent problems. When you're creative, you might be able to express yourself more freely. Additionally, it successfully reduces anxiety. This will lift your spirits and give you a feeling of purpose in addition to giving you a sense of pride and accomplishment. It could be a good idea right now to picture yourself in space, looking down on Earth. Even when the situation looks dire, it may all seem fairly insignificant in comparison to what is happening in the universe.

Chapter

8

Releasing Previous Regrets

Let go of the regret. What we can do is draw lessons from the past and work to avoid repeating the same errors.

Why Should We Forgive? Why is it such a Big Deal?

It takes conscious effort to choose forgiveness when you have unfavorable feelings against someone or yourself. Prior to forgiving, you could feel the following negative emotions: guilt, shame, self-condemnation, humiliation, as well as resentment or bitterness.

Your wellbeing depends critically on your ability to forgive errors or wrongdoings. Learning to forgive "helps individuals hurt less, experience less rage, feel less stress, and suffer less sadness," according to Dr. Frederic Luskin of Stanford University. People who practice forgiveness report much less stress-related symptoms like headaches, dizziness, backaches, and upset stomachs. People often mention changes in their eating, sleeping habits, vitality, and overall wellbeing. You may let go of negativity and concentrate on a more promising future by forgiving both yourself and others.

Why Is Forgiving Oneself So Difficult?

We punish ourselves for previous transgressions much too frequently, as if we could somehow "make up" for the wrong that we've committed. Every day, we go about our business feeling inferior. We label ourselves as failures and bad people. We are bound by our history and harbor sorrows and resentments. And even if no one else is aware of our private suffering, the unfavorable feelings we experience eat away at our happiness and sense of fulfillment in life.

According to therapists and life coaches, it is most difficult to forgive oneself. Not the one who betrayed you, pal. Or the father who didn't stand with you. Even the heartbreaker from your past. Why? Because you are familiar with yourself and regularly interact with yourself. Oh, right.

How to Be Open to Forgiveness

Discuss It

Silence may be dangerous when it comes to the past. So quit playing the part. Break free from the shackles of keeping it all inside, and talk about what's ripping you apart. To a trusted friend, mentor, or counselor, express your feelings. Being open and transparent about your identity—both the good and the bad—is the first step toward forgiveness. Say what you must, then.

Don't Lie to Yourself

We frequently believe, "Maybe if I simply pretend it never occurred, everything will go gone." Nice to hear, but untrue. Make the decision to go past denial and take action. Be forthright about your transgressions and the results of your actions.

Just Accept it as it is

You will have failures in life since you are a flawed being. Admit it. Sometimes, you'll do others harm. You'll feel guilty. It is a natural consequence of existing in a fallen planet. The option is yours, though.

Either you accept your history for what it is or are free to go on and enjoy the present, or your past will keep you stuck in a cycle of guilt and shame. Don't skip out on self-acceptance since it's essential to your emotional wellbeing!

Let Go

Don't cling to your guilt. You don't need to defend your prior choices or make an effort to vindicate yourself. Putting the past to rest entails burying it and renunciation the right to self-criticism.

Both a choice and a process, forgiveness. It involves making the decision to stop devaluing or disliking oneself and start viewing yourself as a valued human being. Getting it out there is one of the first stages towards letting go. Please feel free to let go of anything that has been on your chest for years in the comments section below.

Creating Reasonable Expectations

Examine the standards that you and others have for you. Are they wholesome? Or are they improbable?

You might just need to make a few little adjustments to your way of living if you always fall short, no matter how hard you try. Healthy expectations are not exhausting and overpowering, but rather attainable and satisfying.

Conclusions

Choosing forgiveness when you have negative thoughts against someone or oneself requires intentional effort. You could experience the following unpleasant feelings before forgiving: guilt, shame, self-condemnation, humiliation, as well as anger or bitterness. Too often, we punish ourselves for past wrongdoings, as if we could somehow "make up" for the harm that we've done. Regarding the past, silence might be harmful. Thus, stop acting the part. Talk about the things that are tearing you apart and throw off the chains of holding it all inside. Sometimes we think, "Maybe if I just pretend it never happened, everything will go away." Thoughtful, but false. Decide to take action and get past denial.

Because you are an imperfect person, you will have failures throughout life. Accept it. You could occasionally hurt other people. You will feel bad. Self-acceptance is crucial for your mental health, so don't skip it! Let go of your guilt. You don't need to justify yourself or explain your previous decisions. Burying the past and giving up the right to self-criticism are both necessary steps towards putting it to rest. If you constantly fail, despite your best efforts, you might just need to make a few little changes to your way of life.

Chapter

9

It's Important to Have Some Alone Time

You must first take responsibility for yourself before you can take responsibility for others. Make time for yourself, then. Take advantage of the possibility to reconnect with your body and spirit.

People are innately social beings, and research has demonstrated the importance of social interactions for both mental and physical health. But alone time also has a crucial impact on mental wellness. Although being among others has benefits, it may sometimes be stressful. You stress over what people will say.

To avoid being rejected and blend in with the group, you modify your conduct. Some of these difficulties show why having alone time may be so beneficial, even if they can be the price of living in a sociable environment. You may escape societal demands and access your own ideas, feelings, and experiences when you take some time for yourself.

The COVID-19 epidemic highlighted the difficulties brought on by both loneliness and a shortage of alone time. Others suffered with the difficulties of unexpectedly spending a lot of time in close quarters with family members or housemates, while many individuals fought with feelings of isolation and loneliness.

Many people were suddenly grappling with a complete lack of alone time as a result of blurred work-life boundaries and a lack of time apart.

What Makes Alone Time Important? Finding alone time can offer a lot of significant advantages. A few of these are:

- Personal Investigation
- Creativity
- Social force

Personal investigation

You can have the time and leisure to fully explore your hobbies by learning to be at ease in your own company. It may be a means to explore new interests, learn new information, and even experiment with other ways of expressing yourself.

By allowing yourself some alone time, you may investigate these issues without the constraints and constraints that others could impose. It's essential for growth and personal development to have alone time. Spending time alone allows you to concentrate on your wants and interests rather than worrying about those of others.

Creativity

You may let your thoughts to roam and develop your creativity while you're by yourself. You can disregard outside influences and concentrate inward when you don't need to look out for or communicate with other people. In fact, studies show that being alone may alter the brain in ways that stimulate creativity. According to one research, highly creative individuals also prefer to intentionally retreat in order to spend time alone.

Researchers discovered that perceived social isolation (also known as loneliness) increases activity in the brain circuits connected to imagination in a study published in the journal Nature Communications in 2020. The brain activates its creative networks to assist fill the hole created when there is a lack of social stimulation.

Social Power

Living alone is frequently seen negatively. Researchers have shown that those who live alone may actually have more social energy and a fuller social life than those who share a home.

Things That Take Place When You Are Alone

Our world is one of continual communication, and the value of solitude is being lost in this environment. Rather of working alone at a desk, schoolchildren are put in groups and workplaces are moving away from cubicles in favor of shared workstations and spacious common areas. Our culture seems to have adopted a constant "ping" as its ubiquitous background noise, quickly alerting us to every text, tweet, and notice. Even the simple act of making dinner has gained social media value. The productivity levels of 600 computer programmers at 92 organizations were examined, and it was discovered that while they were generally steady within each organization, they differed substantially between them. The most effective businesses all abandoned the ultra-hip open office in favor of private workplaces that allowed for uninterrupted work. Only 19% of the lowest performers agreed that they had appropriate privacy at work, compared to 62 percent of the best performers. And 76 percent of those who performed poorly stated they were frequently interrupted without cause. The benefits of solitude extend beyond the work realm and include benefits to your mental and emotional health. You must discover the delight of being by yourself if you want to get the most out of life. There are too many advantages of isolation to list them all, but here are some of the finest.

1. You Rest and Replenish

We all need time to rest and rejuvenate, even the hopeless extroverts among us. Spending time alone is the best way to achieve this. You need to be by yourself to feel the calm, quiet, and mental isolation necessary to recover from the strains of daily life.

2. You Can Act Anyway You Choose

Spending time with others is enjoyable, but it always results in compromise.

You're always changing your thoughts to satisfy the needs and preferences of other people. Being by yourself gives you the freedom to do anything you want, whenever you want. You may dress whatever you want to dress, eat however you want to eat, and work on whatever projects you want to work on.

3. You Develop Self-Confidence

Freedom is more than just being able to do what you want; it's the capacity to believe in your instincts and to reason rationally in the absence of external pressure. Being alone yourself enables you to get a clear sense of who you are, what you know, and what is best for you. It instills confidence in you.

You observe other people's responses while you are around them, even if you are not aware of it, to determine whether your own sentiments and actions are suitable. You form your own beliefs and ideas, free from the influence of other people's perspectives. You'll find out what you're actually capable of after you learn to love being by yourself, free from the limitations of other people's perspectives.

4. You Become More Emotionally Intelligent

Your capacity to identify and comprehend your own and others' emotions, as well as how to utilize this understanding to control your behavior and those around you, is known as emotional intelligence (EQ). More than a million people have taken the Talent Smart exam, and the results show that 90% of top achievers have high EQ.

Emotional intelligence is built on self-awareness, and you cannot develop EQ without it. Self-awareness involves rigorous self-reflection, and self-reflection takes place best when you're alone since it necessitates knowing your emotions and how you respond to other individuals and situations.

5. It Improves Your Sense of Self

Being comfortable in your own company greatly boosts confidence. It's simple to begin believing that you're dull or that you require company to have fun if you feel restless and bored when you're by yourself. Alone reassuring you that you are enough, learning to love being by yourself will improve your self-esteem.

6. You are More Appreciative of Others

The saying "absence makes the heart grow fonder" is true. Spending time alone allows you to view individuals in a whole new way and fosters a renewed feeling of thankfulness for both their person and their work.

7. You Accomplish More

While the adage "many hands make light work" may be accurate when it comes to raking leaves, it is quite different when it comes to cognitive activities. Even the value of brainstorming is mostly an urban legend. Because of "cognitive focus," Texas A&M researchers discovered that brainstorming in groups reduces productivity. The bigger the group, the more obsessed everyone becomes. Cognitive fixation is the propensity for people working in groups to become caught on other people's ideas, hindering their ability to come up with anything new. Spending time alone helps you focus by removing distractions and preventing "too many cooks" issues.

Conclusions

Research has shown the significance of social contacts for both mental and physical health since people are inherently social beings. Some of these challenges highlight the potential benefits of spending time alone, even if they may come with living in a social setting. By becoming comfortable in your own company, you can have the time and leisure to completely pursue your interests. It may be a method to discover new interests, gain knowledge, or simply try out different modes of expression. While you're alone yourself, you may let your thoughts to wander and cultivate your creativity.

When you don't have to watch out for or talk to other people, you may ignore outside influences and focus inward. It's common to see living alone negatively. According to studies, those who live alone may actually be more socially active and have a deeper social life than those who live with others. Beyond the sphere of work, isolation has advantages for your mental and emotional well-being. If you want to make the most of life, you must learn to like being by yourself.

Chapter

10

What Is Self-Worth

Never attempt to convince anyone of anything about you. It is not required. Know your value because it will show to others.

The fact is that cultivating traits like self-love, self-esteem, self-empathy, self-regard, and all the other "self" phrases is a terrific and special thing to do. Still, self-worth serves as the cornerstone of them all. Here is a look at how they are all related and some advice on how to begin your road to realizing your own uniqueness.

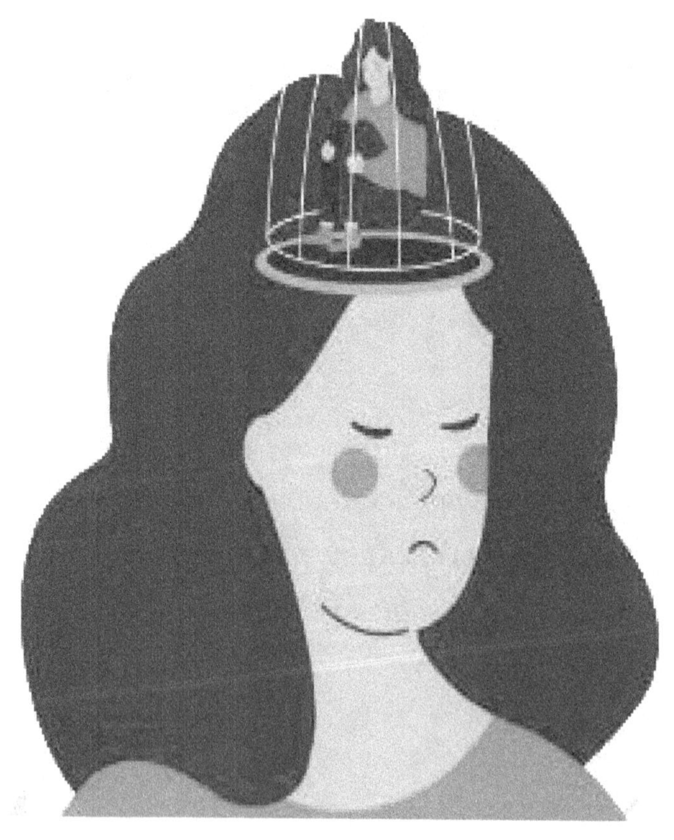

The key to self-awareness is knowing how we define it in our own lives as well as being able to discern between the boxes and labels we may occasionally place ourselves in.

What Is One's Own Worth?

The emphasis you place on yourself might be summed up as your sense of self-worth. Determining how and what you feel about yourself in relation to other people is based on your emotional viewpoint. Your opinion of yourself is one way to define your sense of self-worth. Our sense of self-worth, which governs how we view ourselves, is a basic aspect of who we are.

Everything we consider, feel, and even do is a result of the worth we assign to ourselves on an individual basis. Self-worth is a challenging subject. Here are a few ways to help you identify your own sense of self-worth as it's crucial to do so.

High self-worth individuals accept responsibility for their errors but do not degrade themselves as a result of doing so. When they make a mistake, they state "I did a horrible thing" as opposed to "I am awful." When necessary, they apologize and take steps to put things right.

The Self-Worth Theory

Most people believe that they are only worth something after they have accomplished a goal or when they are in a rivalry. This is the theory: that self-recognition is a person's ultimate objective in life and that it results from their achievements. Additionally, this theory uses aptitude, tenacity, performance, and self-esteem as model components.

These four factors work together to influence how we view ourselves. It may be understandable, but should we really base our self-worth on our achievements to such a great extent? Is the only way we can hold ourselves in high esteem to be better than the next person? What factors contribute the most to one's feeling of worth?

Self-Worth-Defining Elements

People don't only utilize the four criteria from the theory mentioned above to gauge their own value.

Numerous other factors might prevent someone from appreciating their own worth. Some people may be affected by bullying, poor grades, or early trauma. The following are some more typical ways that people assess their own worth:

1. First Line of Contact

Individuals are frequently judged (or judge themselves) based on how many well-known people they are connected to and know.

2. Appearance, both emotional and physical

We often find ourselves making snap decisions about people based just on their appearance—what they wear, how they speak, or how society perceives them.

3. Profession

Another metric people use to assess their own worth is this. For instance, someone could be rude to a waitress while being pleasant to a doctor because they believe the latter is more successful than the former. Career decisions frequently influence a person's life in favorable or bad ways.

4. Belongings

This is a typical metric used to assess one's own worth. The amount of money you make or the kind and quantity of automobiles you possess are just a few examples. Typically, it is tangible assets.

What Self-Worth is not

The fact is that one should never use status or possessions to gauge one's value. Unfortunately, a lot of false beliefs about one's own value have led people to have low opinions of themselves. People often give themselves credit for things that are unrelated to their sense of value.

Career isn't Your Measure of Self-Worth

Your worth of life shouldn't be influenced by your profession. There have been instances where skilled individuals have accepted lowly tasks because they were unable to find employment. Why should a person's sense of worth be determined by their professional choices if doing so doesn't invalidate their qualifications? The job's level of satisfaction is the sole factor that has to be considered.

Self-Worth isn't about What You've Achieved

Achievements are wonderful, but they shouldn't change how important you think of yourself. You shouldn't let a label, certification, or plaque determine your value.

Age is Not a Measure of Self-Worth

Age is just a large number, and I don't intend to seem cliché by saying that, but I will tell you this: Your age has nothing to do with how prepared you are for anything. The world will be at your feet if you are simply willing and committed.

Self-Worth is Not Your Relationship Status

It might be tempting to attempt to feel good about yourself only because someone else does. Imagine if they depart.

Self-Worth is Not Determined by Grades

Are you the student in your class with the lowest IQ? Remember that you are equally as valued as a straight-A student since you have unique talents and could flourish in a different subject that a student with an A average would fail miserably.

You are Not Your Health Status' Self-Worth

Do you have a medical condition that's making you feel down? It is reasonable to state that persons who are optimistic recover more swiftly.

Your Finances do Not Determine Your Level of Worth

Money in and of itself does not define a person. Nothing to be concerned about as long as you are content and have enough to exist.

Self-Worth is Not Related to Your Pickier

Do others consider you to be too smart or old-fashioned for this generation? As long as you are satisfied with who you are, it doesn't matter what they think.

What Is One's Self Worth?

Self-worth just concerns you!

Having to face who "you are" in the absence of material possessions, a desired career, or close relationships can be quite intimidating. Some people find it to be excruciating and will do anything to avoid reaching this point of consciousness. Another very real risk is that someone will start to fear realizing who they are.

It is normal for people to avoid feeling this kind of anxiety or agony. Finding one's self-worth requires this process, which shouldn't ever be ignored. Self-awareness is the initial step in this path, which leads to an eternity of freedom beyond any feeling that appears to be unpleasant.

This is the secret to discovering your worth.

The Value of Self-Worth

Observing the tangible effects it has on your conduct is the finest part of realizing your self-worth. The decisions you make and the actions you take have an impact on your sense of self-worth. You begin to reject anything that alters your perspective on life, and you start to be more receptive to things designed to improve you as a person.

Your sense of self-worth is what keeps you content despite losing all of your accomplishments, assets, and stuff. When you feel good about yourself, life becomes much more meaningful.

How to Acknowledge Your Self-Worth

Having finally realized this, you don't feel good about yourself. Nothing about you excites you. You believe that you are a regular person going about your daily business with nothing remarkable to contribute.

You start to feel as though you require self-worth confirmation. To assess your value as a person, you might wish to do a job or even take a test. You should be aware that self-worth originates inside.

It is the amount of value you place on yourself - by yourself, to restate the thesis of this text. You are enough just by being.

Recovering Strength

Finding your strengths will help you feel more confident about yourself. Every time you begin to doubt your value, these traits will serve as a continual reminder.

You should be able to answer simple questions like "what are my strengths?" and "what makes me unique?" as well as more profound ones like "how have

I benefited others?" and "what problems have I overcome?" These inquiries are where your strength rests.

The Risks of Associating Self-Worth with People and Things

When you keep searching for approval from things and people, you make bad choices. You never get to see yourself as the strong and full of potential individual that you are.

You'll just become frustrated if you seek external affirmation. You prepare yourself for a string of letdowns. Put your internal value first. It is essential for living a healthy lifestyle.

Increasing Your Self-Worth: How to Begin

It's time to discover how to boost, solidify, and maintain your self-worth now that you are aware of the vacuums that are constantly sapping it. Start by identifying the things in which you formerly found value and replace them with more beneficial pursuits.

Here are a few instances:

Whoever Found Self-Worth in School or Their Job

Stop all the excessive reading for a while. Take part in something you really enjoy doing. Pick up a new talent, such as how to play an instrument or salsa dance. Try reading a unique book.

For The Person Who Looked to Social Media for Validation:

For a while, log off. Attend gatherings with active individuals. Exercise outside. Be deliberate in both your speech and deeds. Prove your love and concern for your family and friends. Be there physically for others. Be available to them. Never compare yourself to anybody else while you work to understand your own value. In contrast, you deprive yourself of self-awareness and prevent yourself from realizing your great potential. Comparison merely assesses your value in terms of other people's expectations. Consider coming up with some guidelines on your own.

Let's look at some doable strategies to increase self-worth:

1. Create a Skill or Talent Inventory

Everyone has something valuable to contribute. Humans are endowed with amazing skills that they can learn. Who can you help? Consider your abilities and talents. What wonderful things can you accomplish with ease? By recognizing your strengths, you can stifle your shortcomings and promote your advantages.

2. Observe Yourself

You have to be kind to yourself and accept all of your flaws. Learn from all of your prior errors. You can never feel good about yourself if you constantly feel guilty or humiliated.

3. Take Chances

You haven't done something outstanding for yourself because you are still debating whether you should. Never be scared to take chances in order to improve yourself. Put an end to your self-doubt and go.

If you don't succeed the first time, you'll just have learnt how to succeed the following time. Get up and do action.

4. Love Yourself

Recognize and appreciate who you are. Develop your bad traits by trying to be a better person. Never make the error of denying reality. You would merely put off your release.

5. Make Sure You Are Around Healthy People

Health draws other health. Both positive and harmful behaviors have the potential to spread.

Embrace the change you wish to see in the world. Be among individuals who, like you, have conquered their self-doubts and are on a path to realizing their own value.

Learn How to Surround Yourself with Positive People by reading this chapter. By assessing our self-worth, we may all have healthy lives physically, emotionally, socially, psychologically, and in other ways. We must actively work to increase and enhance our esteem for one another and, more significantly, for ourselves. Deep and long-lasting life happiness comes from having a healthy sense of self-worth.

On your path to understand your worth, it is important to keep in mind that your perspective could alter and you might come to value various things.

Keep surrounding yourself with individuals that encourage your continued progress. Put relationships first that support your new perspective in order to maintain optimism in your life. These are all necessary steps to understanding your own value.

Conclusion

It is a wonderful and exceptional thing to cultivate qualities like self-love, self-esteem, self-empathy, self-regard, and all the other "self" terms. But at their core, they are all built on the concept of self-worth. Your sense of self-worth may be summed up as the importance you place on yourself. Your emotional point of view will determine how and what you feel about yourself in relation to other people. Here are a few techniques to assist you in determining your own sense of value, as doing so is essential. The majority of individuals think that they only have value after achieving a goal or during a rivalry.

Be thoughtful in both your speech and your actions. Show that you care about your friends and family. Be a tangible presence for others. Comparing yourself to others just determines how valuable you are in light of their expectations. Think about developing some rules on your own. Think about your skills and capabilities. What fantastic things are you easily capable of achieving? You may inhibit your weaknesses and boost your advantages by being aware of your strengths. Read this chapter to find out how to surround yourself with positive people. We may all have good lives—physically, emotionally, socially, mentally, and in other ways—by evaluating our own value.

Chapter
11

Sense of

Self-Discipline

The control of thinking is the foundation of self-discipline. You cannot control your needs if you are unable to regulate your ideas.

The key to good leadership, both of yourself and others, is discipline. Focus and self-control lead to contentment, happiness, and success.

When faced with an all-you-can-eat buffet, the chance to make a fast cash, or the sleepy allure of staying in rather than joining the Peloton, it may be difficult to believe, but studies indicate that those with self-discipline are happier. Why? Because when we exercise self-control and discipline, we really achieve more of the objectives that are most important to us.

The link between set objectives and goals achieved is self-discipline. Self-control experts spend less time pondering whether to engage in actions and behaviors that are inconsistent with their beliefs or objectives. They make better decisions. They resist letting emotions or instincts guide their decisions.

They are the designers of their own ideas and the steps they take to bring about a desired result. As a result, they are less susceptible to being sidetracked by temptation and exhibit higher levels of life satisfaction. Not outside events, but your thoughts are under your control. Knowing this will give you courage. You may follow certain steps to develop self-control and the willpower necessary to have a better, more fulfilled life. Self-discipline. Let's be real here. The majority of us are still working on it, despite our best efforts, procrastination, and emotions of failure. But it's not necessary to be. Like anything else, self-control requires practice. Although every day won't be flawless, progress is always being made, and that is what self-discipline is all about. Every day will have its mistakes and minor successes. I've included actions you can take right away to develop self-control. This book provides you with the resources you need to establish a self-discipline practice in all you do, along with some motivation and a sound knowledge of what self-discipline is.

What is Self-Discipline?

Self-discipline is the capacity to carry out your duties. Self-control frequently entails deferring your current comfort or desires in favor of long-term achievement. For instance, to get the long-term benefits of being healthy and feeling wonderful, you could put up with the short-term inconvenience of 5:00 a.m. gym hours. Our emotional mind only prevents us from acting in a way that will help us reach our optimum condition. By taking physical action, self-discipline enables us to override our emotional minds. More than only job advancement is possible with self-discipline. There is proof that it benefits people:

- **Achieve Long-Term Goals**

Self-discipline enables people to reject short-term desires in favor of longer-term, higher-impact objectives. In her 2016 study on persistence and "passion for long-term goals," often known as grit, grit expert Angela Duckworth addresses this. Her research revealed that "the attainment of challenging tasks needs not only skill but also a persistent and focused application of talent over time," or what we would refer to as self-discipline.

- **Reduce Your Anxiousness**

Every one of us has a vice when we're under pressure (Hi, my name is Meg and I procrastinate when stressed). Humans frequently do or think about other things to divert their attention from unpleasant feelings. In fact, a 2016 study discovered that enhancing self-control may aid students in overcoming anxiety-related issues when taking exams.

- **Boost Physical Fitness**

It should go without saying, but those who regularly exercise self-control are more likely to refrain from using harmful drugs like alcohol and cigarettes. Additionally, self-control is associated with decreased incidence of addiction and obesity.

- **Favorably Influence Relationships**

Relationships can benefit from self-control as well. According to Psychology Today, the ability to exercise self-control is a talent for empathic perspective taking, or the capacity to look at things from another person's perspective. By doing these acts, we may overcome our ingrained defensive responses and choose to act in ways that promote better, happier relationships.

- **Increase Your Resiliency**

Do you recover quickly from hardship? Resilience may be predicted by one's level of self-control. It seems that your ability to control your urges and defer pleasure improves with your level of resilience. A resilient person "has a conviction in her own talents to manage life's obstacles and events well," according to Psychology Today.

- **Feel Happier**

Happiness and creativity increase with productivity. The more control we have over the causes of our behavior, the happier we feel and the better off we feel overall!

Know Your Areas of Weakness

Start by outlining your daily activities. After that, consider your values and consider whether your actions are consistent with them. You probably engage in a few daily activities that violate these ideals (hey, we're only human; we all have a few).

It's beneficial to get input from our coworkers, mentors, and family members throughout the identification step. Check to discover whether your self-assessed flaws and how other people see you are similar.

Make a plan of attack once you've decided on a few areas to work on, such as, "One of my weaknesses is to put off calling prospects until it's too late in the day. I'll be behind the remainder of the week because of this, which makes it challenging to achieve my quota.

Recognize Your Strengths

Asking about their evenings, greet your coworkers. To make coffee in the kitchen. Team meal a stroll in the afternoon to the neighborhood café. A lot of time is lost at work as a result of all these little excursions. It's critical to cultivate relationships with coworkers and take regular physical and mental breaks.

However, it's equally crucial to be open and honest about your working habits. It's not a good thing if your mornings are taken up with activities unrelated to your job and that's when you're most productive. Consider your optimum work hours and plan your calendar accordingly.

If your focus is highest between 9:00 a.m. and 12:00 p.m., plan your office coffee breaks at that time. Ensure that you can succeed at work. You'll encourage a better atmosphere for you personally as well as healthier outcomes for your business.

Establish and Record Specific Goals

Did you know that writing down your objectives can increase your chances of achieving them by 42%? Writing down your objectives makes it necessary for you to see them, how to reach them, and the measures you must take to get there. Therefore, before you set out to improve yourself — whether at business or in your personal life — write out your objectives.

Imagine the results you want

Your brain cannot tell the difference between actual and made-up memories. As a result, when you intensely picture something, your brain chemistry alters just as you had a real experience. You may experience the good sensations associated with rising to the top of the leaderboard while lowering feelings of uneasiness by visualizing positive outcomes, such as, "When I make it to the top of our activity board, I'm going to treat myself to an exquisite meal." This makes it simpler for you to get over your fears and take meaningful moves in the direction of your objectives.

Never Wait till It Seems Right

You risk never beginning the task that needs to be done if you hold off until everything is just right, including your schedule, workplace, and inbox. Accept that every instant has all you require in order to perform at your best because, well, it does.

Small at First

Motivated by this list? Are you prepared to break negative behaviors and become the best salesperson or employee possible? Begin modestly. A week-long overhaul of your work habits can only lead to exhaustion and failure. Choose a few manageable behaviors to work on each week instead. You could choose to carry your coffee to work for the first week in order to skip the "break room morning's rabbit hole and instead start working straight away.

After a successful week, you could block off a portion of your Friday afternoon to complete administrative activities like entering prospect notes into the CRM or responding to unanswered emails. You could surprise yourself with how much more productive and disciplined you've become after a few weeks of enhancing one behavior at a time.

Find a Mentor

There are some topics you can broach with a mentor that you would not feel confident doing so with a coworker or management. I might feel comfortable challenging my mentor than my boss if I want to quit wasting so much time on social media when I could be prospecting.

Mentors often have more experience, are familiar with you, and can provide you with the frank comments and guidance you need to thrive not only in your present position but throughout your whole career.

Try, Fail, and Try Again

Self-disciplined people don't always have days where they consume all the doughnuts in the kitchen, spend 45 minutes on social media, and lose two prospects before 10:00 a.m. They act in this way, then when they awaken the following morning, they attempt to make wiser choices. The act of attempting, failing, and trying again is self-discipline.

Understand how you'll gauge your success

It will be challenging to determine your success if you don't have a plan for monitoring your development. Start by deciding how many appointments you want to schedule in the first half of the month if your objective is to book more meetings. Determine how many meetings you'll need each week and how long it will take for each one to be finished, then work backward from there.

Establish what success looks like once you've figured out the specifics of your objective. Are you just trying to hit the total? If a meeting is called off last-minute, would it still count? A demo should follow the meeting, right? Establish the parameters of success so you can quantify it.

Consider Your Own Health

When you are torturing yourself to develop self-control, it is of very little use. Everybody works the rare 28-hour day (you know such exist), but if you spend weeks or months staying up late in an effort to be more "self-disciplined," you've missed the purpose.

Taking care of oneself is a crucial component of self-control. The world— and we— revolve around breaks throughout the day, a wholesome diet, lots of sleep, and good relationships. According to research, mindfulness practices like taking a little stroll, observing five things around you, or naming two odors can really boost employee productivity.

Enjoy Yourself

Want your positive habits to last? Self-rewarding is important, according to studies. When we are deprived, we begin to excuse undesirable behavior. This phrase, which sounds like "I've earned this" or "I deserve this," frequently signals the start of our advances' decline.

Give yourself rewards as you develop self-control instead. Whether it's a fancy meal or a new pair of shoes, these delights will make you feel energized, revived, and never deprived.

Pardon Yourself.

Furthermore, you must be willing to accept responsibility for your mistakes. You will fail, as we discussed in point eight; this is a given. It's crucial that you go past this. To accomplish that, you must first forgive yourself. It's not about giving yourself permission to fall short, as my wonderful boss Emma

Brudner recently informed me. Realistic perception of everything is the goal.

Look at the issue realistically if you wake up late, rush to the office, and forget to bring your coffee, forcing you down the break room rabbit hole for 30 minutes of colleague discussion and three prospect calls shy of your day objective.

Will you need to make any further calls on Monday? Probably. Will this affect your long-term progress in any way? Nope. You can choose how to proceed and resume your course once you've considered the effects of your slip. Just before going to bed, make sure your alarm is set.

Self-discipline requires work, keep in mind. You won't always be flawless. It's crucial to arrive each day prepared to attempt.

Conclusion

Discipline is the secret to effective leadership, both of yourself and of others. Success, happiness, and fulfillment follow self-control and focus. The ability to do your obligations is a sign of self-discipline. Delaying your current comfort or pleasures in favor of long-term success is a common example of self-control. People typically engage in other activities or think about unfavorable emotions in order to distract themselves. Self-control is also helpful in relationships. Self-control is a skill for empathetic perspective taking, or the capability to see things from another person's perspective, according to Psychology Today. Self-control ability is a predictor of resilience. Productivity boosts happiness and creativity. During the identification phase, it is helpful to get feedback from our coworkers, mentors, and family members.

By putting your goals in writing, you are forced to consider how to achieve them as well as the essential steps. Holding off on starting the assignment until your schedule, workplace, and inbox are all exactly right puts you at danger of never doing it. Start off subtly. If you don't have a strategy for tracking your progress, it will be hard to evaluate your success. It serves very little use when you are torturing yourself to learn self-control. Instead, reward yourself as you learn self-control. Keep in mind that developing self-discipline takes effort. You won't constantly be faultless. It's important to come prepared to work every day.

Chapter

12

Growing Your Growth Mindset

In order to progress, extend yourself, and develop your talents, you must have a growth mentality.

A fixed mindset, or a mindset that considers abilities and talents are given, constrained, and only marginally amenable to change, is frequently what prevents a person from succeeding. This individual thinks that their traits, both good and bad, were predetermined at birth and that they remain mostly fixed throughout life. While they often understand the need of education and training, they frequently lack the ability to expand their horizons and envision a brave and radically different future.

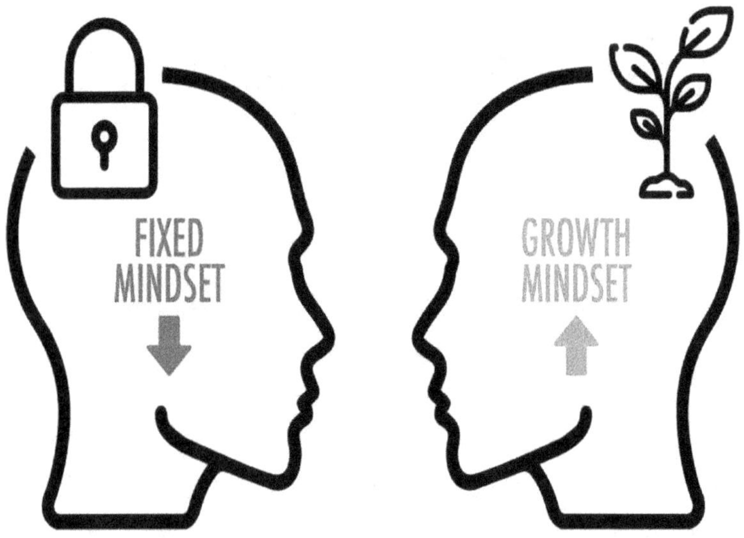

On the other hand, a growth mentality is one that is always evolving and working to improve, develop, and hone all innate qualities and gifts as well as supplementing and upgrading those gained along the way.

Those of us who have a growth mindset may develop and strengthen talents and abilities to do things that were formerly considered to be impossible given time, effort, and practice. You don't simply believe this if you have a development mindset; you really do it. According to what is believed to be Henry Ford, "Whether you believe you can do a thing or not, you are right."

Ford understood that the idea that you can't accomplish something will hold you back more than anything else. He didn't use the word "fixed mentality," but he surely could have if it had been in use at the time. He could have also identified a stuck thinking as a source of sadness.

The Advantages of a Growth Mindset

People who have a growth mindset are more likely to welcome difficulties, make use of criticism, and move on from mistakes and setbacks than those who don't.

Learning new things will be enjoyable for someone with a development mentality. As a result, they will be willing to face obstacles and persistent in their pursuit of their objectives. Because they are more prone to seek solutions tenaciously, this can encourage creativity.

Someone with a development mentality won't feel intimidated by the brilliance and success of others since they are more concerned with improving themselves than defending themselves. Instead, kids will be more inclined to look up to, learn from, and be inspired by others.

Problems with a Fixed Mindset

Because they present a direct challenge to the ego, learning experiences are more likely to be avoided by those with fixed mindsets. Attending a class, for example, becomes less about learning and more about seeking for a chance to prove that they already know all the answers since the stakes of success and failure are substantially raised by the ego's urge to defend itself. A person with a fixed mindset is more prone to shy away from difficulties, give up easily, and think it is pointless to put up effort in pursuit of a goal.

An Evolutionary Approach to Freedom

As opposed to being constrained by limiting ideas, a growth mindset gives you greater flexibility to realize your full potential and stay true to your principles. The possibilities are endless with this freedom. Additionally, it gives one the bravery and inspiration to try something new, fail, and try again. That who enjoy this kind of freedom think they have the power to alter not just their own lives but also those of others. They don't believe that anything is static.

How to Develop a Growth Mindset Practically

Both mindsets are the result of a lifetime of learning, experiences, and observations. But you can create a growth mentality with work, practice, and commitment. Here are some helpful actions:

- You must first have confidence in your ability. Use a mantra or other comparable tool every day. Persuade yourself that you are capable of making all the necessary modifications. To inculcate this in yourself could need some effort, but if you keep in mind the benefits of development and achievement, you can succeed.

- Don't assign blame to events or other people for your failings. You must understand that you are in charge of shaping your own destiny and maximizing your natural talents and abilities. Therefore, the next time you catch yourself placing blame, take a step back, accept responsibility, recognize the lesson, and then move on.

- Change-seekers must also be inquisitive. Observe how little you know. Get accustomed to this sensation. The unknown should thrill rather than instill dread or humiliation. Ask inquiries and look for further information to follow up on it.

- Let yourself struggle. It's imperative that you attempt and fail, then try again, as difficult as that may be. Every setback serves as a learning experience that leads to success. I'm sure I don't need to mention the several well-known figures who initially failed horribly before rising to prominence as role models, leaders, and influencers.

- Step outside of your comfort zone and learn to operate there. The comfort zone serves as a haven for many of us, a place to escape difficulties. To be "free from obstacles" is to be "free from progress," nevertheless. Push yourself to advance.

- Keep a watch out for jealousy, the green-eyed monster. Think, "I'll utilize their success as a model for what I want to achieve," rather than, "Boy, do I wish I had achieved what they have," when you see someone else succeed. The former encourages success, whereas the latter restricts it. You may use appreciation as a tool to lead you toward achievement.

- Finally, don't let your ego's need for protection stand in the way of the adjustments that might improve your happiness and prosperity. You will be pushed by a growth mentality to take on challenges that make you feel less confident, less successful, and more fearful. Although the ego dislikes this, giving in to it can only lead to mediocrity. You must be ready to confront your ego, limiting beliefs, and presumptive limits if you wish to flourish and achieve.

Your emotional intelligence may help you tremendously in developing a development attitude. Continue reading to learn how to use emotional intelligence to overcome the stuck mindset's sadness trigger and open the door to success in every aspect of your life.

Conclusion

A fixed mindset, or a mindset that believes skills and capabilities are predetermined, limited, and mostly immutable, is typically what stands in the way of success. A growth mindset allows you more freedom to fulfill your full potential and adhere to your values rather than restricting you with limiting concepts. To start, you must believe in your own abilities. Change-seekers need to be curious as well. Keep in mind how little you know. Let yourself to battle. No matter how challenging it may be, you must try something, fail, and try again. Don't blame situations or other people for your mistakes. You can find it quite helpful to create a growth mindset if you have high emotional intelligence.

Chapter

13

Fostering Empathy

The ability to generate community compassion is humanity's greatest skill.

The ability to see things from another person's perspective and put oneself in their shoes is the foundation of empathy. However, it goes beyond that ability. While actors, politicians, salespeople, and marketers are frequently highly adept at seeing things from several angles, they cannot care about other people.

Torturers and con men adopt different viewpoints in order to prey on people's vulnerabilities. Empathy involves appreciating various viewpoints and individuals. Compassion and perspective-taking are key.

How do parents foster empathy? Here are five recommendations based on research and the experience of practitioners.

1. Show your youngster empathy and exhibit empathy for others.

Children pick up empathy through seeing us and by feeling it when we are kind toward them. Children form safe, trustworthy ties with us when we sympathize with them. These bonds are crucial to their desire to embrace our beliefs and behave in a manner similar to ours, which will help them develop empathy for others.

The ability to empathize with our children can take many different forms, such as being aware of their emotional and physical needs, respecting and understanding each child's unique personality, showing a sincere interest in their lives, and directing them toward activities that are in line with who they are as individuals and what they find enjoyable.

Children can develop empathy by observing the people we value and notice. If we act as though a mailman or a waitress at a restaurant are invisible, people will notice. On the plus side, they will take note if we welcome a new family to our child's school or show care for a different child in our child's class who is having some difficulties.

Finally, it's critical for us to understand any potential obstacles to empathy. For instance, are we stressed or exhausted? Does our kid have a tendency to set us off in a way that makes parenting them challenging at times?

Recognize your kid. You should question your child. For instance, what intriguing information did you discover today? What was the most challenging time of the day? If you could do anything for a day, how would you like to spend it the most? Do you have a buddy whom you hold in the highest regard? Why do you regard that individual?

Empathize with people, including those who are different from you. Think about routinely performing volunteer work or serving your community in different ways. Consider doing this with your child to make it even better. Show interest in people from varied backgrounds who are dealing with a wide range of difficulties.

2. Prioritize helping others and establish high standards for ethical behavior.

It's crucial for kids to learn from their parents that compassion for others is a high priority and that it is just as vital as their own pleasure if they are to appreciate other people's viewpoints and act compassionately toward them. Even though the majority of parents claim that having kind children is their top priority, kids frequently don't get that message.

Keep your message concise. Think about the lessons you provide to kids every day about the value of kindness. For instance, you may say "The most important thing is that you're nice and that you're happy" rather than "The most essential thing is that you're happy."

When speaking with other significant individuals in your children's life, put compassion first. For instance, in addition to inquiring about your children's academic achievement, grades, or talents, ask instructors and coaches if they are compassionate members of the community.

Assist your kids in realizing that everything is not about them. It's important for parents to sometimes put their children's concern for others before their own happiness, such as when they demand that kids turn off the TV and assist around the home, act politely even when they're upset, or keep their voices down while speaking to other kids or adults.

3. Give youngsters the chance to exercise empathy.

Although empathy is a talent that children are born with, it must be developed throughout the course of their lives. In some ways, developing empathy is similar to learning a language or a sport. It needs instruction and practice. Through trial and error, youngsters can improve their ability to tune into the sentiments and viewpoints of others by regularly contemplating other people's perspectives and circumstances.

Family gatherings when there are difficulties or disagreements in the family, call family meetings. At these sessions, let the kids speak out and urge them to consider the viewpoints of other family members. Ask your children to listen intently to other people's viewpoints as well as your own.

Encourage your classmates to show empathy. Children should be questioned about their friends and classmates. Encourage kids to take their peers' viewpoints into account when they are at odds with their classmates.

Think about compassion and empathy. When you and your kid are together, pay attention to instances where someone demonstrates significant empathy—or a lack of empathy—either in real life, in a book, or on television. Discuss the value of empathetic behavior and the dangers of missing it.

Discuss moral conundrums. Talk with your child with moral conundrums so they may understand other viewpoints, such as "Should I welcome a new neighbor to my birthday party when my best buddy doesn't like her?" If I find out that my friend's boyfriend, who is also my friend, cheated on her, should I inform her?

Encourage doing with. Encourage kids to solve problems in the community by working with varied student groups rather than merely performing acts of service or doing things "for" other people.

4. Increase the area of worry for your youngster.

We frequently refer to empathy as a numerical value. As an illustration, we describe youngsters as having a lot, a little, or no empathy at all. However, it's not always a question of whether or how much empathy youngsters have. It's the people they feel sympathy for. Empathy is often not difficult for most of us to feel for our loved ones and close friends. Humans naturally have a soft spot in their hearts for those who resemble ourselves in some manner.

However, the fundamental question is whether kids (and adults) can feel empathy outside of that small group. It's crucial for parents and caregivers to demonstrate appreciation for a variety of individuals. It's crucial that we teach kids how to respect and care for a variety of individuals who are different from them and who can be dealing with difficulties totally dissimilar from their own.

In and out the lens. Encourage them to zoom in, paying close attention to others, as well as out, taking in a variety of viewpoints and individuals. Start discussions with kids about other people's struggles and difficulties or just the various experiences of kids in a different nation or town by using newspaper or television articles.

The true challenge, however, is to comprehend individuals who are unique or in need. Instill in your child the value of paying attention to others, even those who may appear strange or whose words they may not comprehend right away. Encourage kids to take into account the sentiments of others who could be weak, such as a kid going through a difficult home situation or a kid who isn't well liked. Give them some straightforward suggestions for taking action, such as consoling a friend who has been bullied.

Encourage kids to regulate their emotions and develop self-discipline.

Often, it's not because kids lack empathy that they don't show it. It's because something is preventing them from feeling empathy. Often, unpleasant emotions such as wrath, humiliation, jealousy, or other ones prevent us from being able to care for others. What "releases" children's empathy is frequently helping them manage these unfavorable emotions as well as preconceptions and prejudices about others.

Determine Emotions

Children's tough emotions, such as frustration, sadness, and anger, should be named for them, and you should urge them to discuss them with you.

Self-Control in 3 Easy Steps

Practice these three basic techniques with your child: pause, take a deep breath with your nose, and exhale through your mouth. Then, count to five. When your kids are calm, give it a try. When you notice that they are becoming agitated, go over the steps with them and practice them together.

Resolve Disputes

Teach your youngster conflict resolution skills via practice. Think about a confrontation that you or your kid saw or experienced that went poorly, and role-play several responses. If your youngster notices you feeling uncomfortable and is worried, explain to them how you are addressing it.

Conclusion

Empathy is built on the capacity to perceive things from another person's perspective and put oneself in their shoes. It extends beyond that capability, though. Through witnessing the individuals we admire and pay attention to, children can learn empathy. People will notice if we act as if a mailman or a server at a restaurant are invisible. To make it even better, think about doing this with your child. Take an interest in people from various origins who are facing a variety of challenges. Keep your remarks brief. Consider the lessons you teach children about the need of kindness every day. Help your children understand that nothing is about them in the world. Instruct your kids to pay close attention to both your own and other people's points of view.

Humans typically use a number to represent empathy. For instance, we categorize children as having a lot, some, or no empathy. Kids frequently don't exhibit empathy for others not because they lack it. It's because they are unable to empathize for whatever reason. Name difficult feelings that children experience, such as frustration, sadness, and anger, and encourage them to talk to you about them. Practice conflict resolution techniques with your child.

Chapter

14

The Power of Intrinsic Motivation

Fear and rewards both have the power to inspire. These two approaches, however, are only transitory. Self-motivation is the only thing that lasts.

Let's look at the American Psychological Association's definition of intrinsic motivation for a start:

An urge to engage in a particular activity that stems from enjoyment of the action rather than from any potential external advantages is known as intrinsic motivation. By extension, internal motivation is when you do something because you find it intriguing, gratifying, or delightful on the inside. When acting out of personal motivation, you don't look to others for approval or praise.

Why Internal Motivation Is Superior than External Motivation

To be motivated is to feel moved to do action.

In general, inspiration is something we all need. Internal incentives are significantly more effective than extrinsic rewards when it comes to finding the long-term urge to "do something," according to a significant body of research in the field.

Why? It's easy. When you do something because "you want to," as opposed to "you must," there is a significant difference.

Just consider the most straightforward illustration there is: labor.

How much happiness will you gain from your job if you drag your feet and hate going in to work each day? What about output and outcomes? Work's quality?

You will not soon be at the top of the list for Employee of the Month, you are correct. External motivation has the drawback of being fleeting.

It is vulnerable to a phenomenon that psychologists refer to as hedonic adaptation. The phrase "external rewards are not a sustainable source of happiness and contentment" is used informally. How long does your "high" stay after working 100-hour weeks in order to advance?

According to research, the sensation of being on a cloud swiftly passes, leaving you craving more. As a result, you are trapped on a never-ending "hedonic treadmill," meaning that you can never stop being inspired by larger and better things only to discover that, when you do eventually obtain them, they don't provide you with the satisfaction you were hoping for.

Or, to put it as brilliantly as novelist and journalist Oliver Burkeman does: "Write every day" won't work unless you want to write. And if you don't at least somewhat love what you're doing, no workout program will survive very long.

Advantages of Internal Motivation

According to studies, intrinsic motivation consistently outperforms extrinsic motivation as a long-term predictor of work success.

One explanation is that when we are inwardly motivated to do something, we only do it because we love it. We continue to work each day because we are motivated, inspired, joyful, and content with who we are.

Another explanation is that behaviors that are inwardly driven are linked to things like greater purpose, giving to a good cause, or doing for reasons other than our own or our own gain. According to research, using external motivators like praise impairs students' internal drive and ultimately leads to "slower skill development and more learning mistakes."

Children who are intrinsically motivated, on the other hand, are more invested in the job at hand, like it more, and purposefully seek out obstacles. The conclusion drawn from all the study is that intrinsic motivation is essential if you want to avoid the drudgery we occasionally experience when deciding what to do or must accomplish.

How to Unlock Your Internal Motivation

Imagine you had a ditch to dig. Many people could view this as a task that they would either not enjoy doing or would only do if they were paid to do it. Both of which, if you've been paying attention, are extrinsic motivators. But what if you were constructing a swimming pool out of the ditch that would provide you and your family years of enjoyment? For you and the majority of people, this would undoubtedly change things.

These may seem to be extrinsic ideas, but they are a type of "growth motivation," as defined by psychologist Abraham Maslow as motivation that comes from sources other than fundamental necessities. As it did for me, it is a genuinely amazing location that will bring you years of prosperity and fulfillment. But how, I hear you ask? Here are five fast ideas to get your intrinsic motivation going:

- Start by taking a comprehensive look at each challenge or scenario you are faced with.
- Separate it into its component parts, why, how, and what.
- Pay attention to the component that will make you feel happy or satisfied within.
- Make this the focal point of the project.
- Consider your blessings and try to be grateful for everything, if not just this part.

How to Improve Your Internal Motivation

So, how does one increase the positive stuff, or how does one develop internal motivation? You may do a lot of things to increase your drive. The list's top candidates are listed below.

Efficacy in Oneself

The self-efficacy hypothesis was created in 1982 by American psychologist Albert Bandura of Canadian descent.

Efficacy is our self-belief in our ability to accomplish the objectives we set for ourselves.

To put it another way, it's about whether we believe we "have what it takes" to succeed at what we do. The relationship between self-efficacy and improved performance, increased drive, and higher self-esteem is clear. High self-efficacy individuals are more likely to exert additional effort, set more difficult objectives for themselves, and be more motivated to develop their talents.

Therefore, having confidence in our abilities acts as a self-fulfilling prophesy, encouraging us to work more in order to demonstrate our abilities to ourselves.

Connect Your Behavior to a Greater Goal

Discovering your life's "why" is crucial. This means that you need to be certain about your motivations and the reasons behind your actions.

What do you find inherently rewarding? It's known as "reframing your story" in psychology.

Do you recall the well-known tale about John F. Kennedy's trip to NASA in 1961? He met a janitor there and inquired about his position at NASA, as the story goes. "I'm trying to get a man on the Moon," was the response. It's motivating, isn't it? An effective motivator and meaning-maker is rephrasing your goals in terms of how they will benefit others and leave a lasting impression on the cosmos.

Volunteer

A fantastic method to give back to the world is via volunteering. By giving you a sense of importance in helping those who are less fortunate, acquiring new skills, feeling good about yourself, or connecting to some of your inner values, like compassion and humanitarianism, it may also assist increase your internal drive. When you put aside all external reward expectations and act only out of joy and contentment in helping others, you are acting with intrinsic motivation.

Don't wait to act till you "feel like it"

We often say things like, "I can't force myself go to the gym," or "I can't get up early," but what we really mean is that we don't feel like it, according to a wonderful article in the Harvard Business Review.

Apart from our lethargy, nothing psychically hinders us from taking those actions.

The truth is that you don't need to "feel like it" in order to act.

Sometimes you might not want to accomplish anything at first, but once you get going, you get into the flow and discover your innate motivation.

Choosing oneself (As I Call It)

Richard Ryan and Edward Deci, two psychology professors from the University of Rochester, developed the self-motivation hypothesis in the middle of the 1980s.

One of the most well-known theories in the area of motivation, it focuses on the various forces that influence human behavior, including inner and extrinsic motivators. The idea goes on to say that we might achieve our desire for growth by satisfying three primary needs: competence, autonomy, and relatedness (CAR).

Our performance will increase if our occupations provide us the opportunity to learn and develop, and if we have the freedom to act independently and creatively.

Humans are social creatures, thus we also need to feel appreciated and connected to others.

These intrinsic motivational factors can be strong motivators to keep us thriving even when we don't feel inspired or driven, both individually and collectively.

Go Deeper with Your Reason

How high-performing individuals maintain their motivation when their employer is unable or unwilling to participate in intrinsic or extrinsic motivational strategies was the subject of an intriguing study conducted in 2016.

The study followed employees at a Mexican plant where they performed the same jobs every day with almost little opportunity to advance professionally or gain new skills. No of how well they performed, everyone received the same pay. Therefore, the only intrinsic drive was to maintain one's employment.

The third type of motivation was later identified and was dubbed "family motivation" by researchers. Although they had no additional internal or external motivation to do so, employees who agreed more with statements like "I care about providing for my family" or "It is crucial for me to do good for my family" were more motivated and performed better.

This type of driver has the advantage of being unconstrained by one's employer or circumstance. It touches on a deeper truth: if you don't want to accomplish something for yourself, do it for the people you care about. And as many people can certainly confirm, this is a strong motivation.

When it comes to boosting our general well-being and finding long-term enjoyment and satisfaction in all we do, intrinsic motivation tips the scales.

The next time you need a little motivation to get anything done, remember to tie it to an overarching objective, preferably one that provides non-financial rewards.

Remember the NASA janitor when you're feeling down or unsure of how to create motivation within yourself. You will be absolutely unstoppable once you discover your internal generator, so do it now.

Conclusion

Intrinsic motivation is the desire to do something out of delight rather than because of any prospective benefits from outside sources. Studies show that as a long-term predictor of performance at work, intrinsic drive regularly performs better than extrinsic motivation. On the other side, youngsters who are genuinely driven are more immersed in the task at hand, like it more, and deliberately seek out challenges. One of the most well-known theories in the field of motivation, it focuses on the different factors, including intrinsic and extrinsic motivators, that affect people's behavior. When you're feeling depressed or unsure of how to inspire yourself, think about the NASA janitor.

Chapter

15

Feedback Management

Instead of being pondered over and preserved, mistakes should be investigated, learnt from, and eliminated.

Any leader's skill set must include feedback. This talent is developed during the course of a person's career by project managers, team leaders, teachers, and coaches. For effective information sharing among teams and organizations, feedback must be given as well as received. Examining its worth in greater detail will help us understand how to deliver it more effectively.

Constructive criticism is a powerful tool for improving performance, fostering a positive work atmosphere, and increasing engagement and productivity. In a variety of sectors, it has a good impact on collaborative outcomes, communication, and member interaction.

It is difficult to overstate the value of feedback in the workplace: exchanging knowledge about what needs to be improved and what can be optimized speeds up and streamlines work processes.

- In leadership and communication, feedback is very beneficial since it enhances openness and paints a clear picture.
- By facilitating the quicker assimilation of new information and preventing the repetition of errors, feedback is essential to education and learning.
- In sports and coaching, feedback also aids in learning new techniques and improving outcomes.

The Value of Recommendations

So what precisely makes feedback so great? Let's see how it might be applied by team leaders to affect collaboration and effort inside their team or group.

Everyone Stays On Course with Feedback

Everyone engaged in any kind of activity, such as working on a project, getting ready for an occasion, learning, etc., would benefit from it.

Feedback Aids in Preventing Costly Errors on Your Team

Any sort of cooperation benefits from having open and honest communication since it eliminates the need to spend time correcting someone else's work, minimizes mistakes due to misunderstandings, and stops individuals who believe they failed from feeling remorse.

You Build Stronger Connections

Feedback encourages openness and confidence. It frequently entails criticism, which most people find uncomfortable.

Feedback Fosters Progress On both a Personal and Professional Level

In order to improve performance, it is important to actively listen, take the time to evaluate, and then come up with the best answer. It offers constructive feedback and enables people to identify what they can alter to sharpen their attention and achieve better achievements. It facilitates interpersonal interaction and good communication.

Getting Feedback Promotes a Welcoming Workplace

Other beneficial outcomes that greatly benefit you are an eagerness to seek input and an openness to criticism. The finest solutions frequently come from team members who merely bring up a potential fix or draw attention to a problem that others haven't yet seen.

Feedback Has Some Immediate Advantages for Company

They include business expansion, cost savings, increased sales, on-time project completion, and other favorable improvements to the company's finances, customer connections, and market positioning.

All of this increases team members' involvement in the work process. Once providing feedback becomes a regular practice, you could discover people grow more engaged and devoted.

The Capability of Giving Feedback

The value of feedback for a team leader, boss, or instructor cannot be overstated. It is a strong technique that has a definite good impact, but it may also be harmful, undermine someone's self-worth, or make them feel unappreciated.

Plan your strategy in advance to do this task correctly. Take into consideration some straightforward suggestions about how to provide and receive criticism.

First off, steer clear of anything that can be seen as criticism or condemnation; instead, try to inspire others by pointing out areas in which they might grow. Always demonstrate to your staff the benefits of open conversation regarding potential improvements. Mention their advantages first, then a weakness they should focus on improving.

Be sure to be descriptive and include examples. Your team members need to understand precisely the project component you're referring to, what went wrong, and how it might be fixed. Use of objective data, such as time monitoring and employee progress statistics, which show how much time each person needs to accomplish tasks and what activities they participate in along the way, is crucial for this reason. You may use it to gather information for your feedback and track team performance in real time.

Give them time to comprehend your criticism, and be sure to get their comments back. They ought to feel at ease talking about their feelings. Consider the perspectives of your teammates and have an open mind.

Don't forget to involve them in the solution of the problem. Even if you already have a solution in mind, listen to what they have to say before sharing your suggestion utilizing some of their words or concepts.

It happens frequently that individuals are unsure of what occurred or what to do next. Because of this, you should check to determine if the other person understood your message by asking questions at the conclusion. Check in with them a few days later to check how they are doing and whether the problem is still there.

Last but not least, motivate team members to provide their own opinions. Leave your ego at the door, ask them if they have any more comments regarding your work or your position as boss, and pay close attention to what they have to say.

Allow them to provide examples as well so you can fully understand what they mean. Then, discuss this openly and collaboratively to come up with a solution and utilize the input.

The Value of Recommendations

Your subsequent action should be to encourage team input. Make time (and room) for it when organizing your next activities.

Consider the fact that feedback ought to be provided at every stage. Allow your employees some time to adjust to this brand-new, accommodating workplace.

Conclusion

Each leader must possess the ability to provide feedback. Project managers, team leaders, professors, and coaches help people develop this talent throughout their careers. An effective strategy for raising productivity, encouraging a good work environment, and enhancing performance is constructive criticism. Everyone involved in any activity, including studying, completing a project, preparing for an event, etc., would gain from it. Feedback promotes confidence and transparency.

It often involves criticism, which most people find upsetting. To do this work correctly, prepare your approach in advance. Give them some time to absorb your critique, and be sure to solicit their feedback. Kids should feel comfortable discussing their emotions.

Encourage team members to contribute their own viewpoints last but not least. Put your ego aside, ask them if they have any more feedback about your job or your role as the boss, and pay attentive attention to what they have to say. Consider the requirement that input be given at each level. Give your staff some time to get accustomed to this modern, friendly environment.

Chapter

16

Communication Clarification

Use every chance to improve your communication abilities so that when crucial situations happen, you will be equipped with the talent, the mannerisms, the clarity, the emotions, and the sharpness to influence others. The fullness of life is unlocked through gratitude.

One of the most crucial abilities you may develop is the capacity for good communication. But communicating clearly and concisely isn't the only thing that's required. Additionally, it involves being able to adapt and comprehend how other individuals communicate differently.

.One of the coveted soft talents for 2019 was said to be how to adapt to various personalities, but doing so takes a high level of emotional intelligence.

What precisely are the various communication styles then? How do you deal with each of them? What should you stay away from? You can trust us.

The True Cost of Poor Communication

Have you ever had a conversation at work with someone and felt that they simply didn't get what you were trying to say? Naturally, you have. Since everyone has a unique communication style and not everyone is aware of how to modify their own to fit the needs of others. Working with diverse personalities is exactly what occurs; neither you nor they are to blame. But there are negative effects.

Lost Time

First off, when communication styles diverge, conversations—both online and offline—tend to drag on longer. Everyone gets more frustrated as more explanation is required, tempers are tried, and more emails are written. The immediate drawback of incompatible communication styles is this.

Erroneous Errors

A dreadful thing frequently occurs when two individuals are having problems communicating: They begin speculating. They frequently give up after repeatedly seeking clarification and merely attempt to follow the unclear directions. This typically necessitates further modifications later on.

Strained Relations

Nobody enjoys being misunderstood, and two people who have previously had trouble coordinating their communication styles will avoid working together in the future. This has a significant negative impact on productivity and morale in offices with a variety of personalities (as most do and should). Teams function best when members respect and accommodate one another's differences.

Why Improved Communication Is Beneficial To You (And Your Team)

Less time is lost. Check! Better connections. Double-check! Employees who are more centered, relaxed, and content? Of course.

We may accomplish more and do so with less stress and angst if we are aware of our various communication styles. And for collaboration, that can only be a good thing.

Why Clarification is Important at Work

Every one of us has occasionally had to follow vague, ambiguous, or imprecise directions. These hazy directions may be perplexing, which may lead to mistakes, misunderstandings, and low team morale.

Inquiring About Something

Asking for clarification is crucial if your employer or supervisor communicates in a confusing manner. In order to avoid misunderstandings during meetings, projects, or the scope of work, it is important to communicate assertively to make sure you completely grasp what is expected of you.

Clarification improves teamwork, communication, and organizational culture.

The Need for Clarification

Here are five reasons and instances for why we should be ready to provide clarification when requested:

1. To prevent Disagreement at work

Agreeing to something you're unsure of often leads to misunderstandings, which is one of the factors that lead to conflict at work. Each partner must be aware of the implications of their participation, how their actions affect other people's work, and what is expected of them before agreeing to projects or assignments.

2. To avoid being under or overworked.

More responsibilities and projects are given to you as you become more fully involved in your profession. Always remember to ask questions when your immediate boss, supervisor, or team leader assigns you tasks that are not part of your normal job. Audit your tasks and establish priorities. Request a change in the deadlines if you believe that adding additional task might jeopardize your current work. Ask for permission to put off your existing responsibilities if something has to be done right now and is urgent. If not, ask someone else to do it or assign some of your task to someone else.

3. To make certain that everyone in the Team is on the Same Page

The most crucial components of team meetings are idea sharing and question asking. The team will be able to develop a common understanding of their position in the project or work at hand by asking questions and setting clear expectations. By setting clear expectations, clarifying ensures that everyone in the team is on the same page.

4 To avoid making assumptions that could lead to subpar performance.

Decisions based on assumptions or activities carried out without clear instructions frequently lead to inefficiency and project failure. Knowing what is expected of you before taking any projects or assignments is crucial and lowers your chance of making mistakes. Decisions based on assumptions or activities carried out without clear instructions frequently lead to inefficiency and project failure. Knowing what is expected of you before taking any projects or assignments is crucial and lowers your chance of making mistakes. Do not be afraid to inquire and explain if you believe the instructions are unclear or if you require further information from any member of the team.

5. To prevent misunderstandings, which might result in errors and project overruns

One of the main reasons projects go wrong is poor communication in the workplace. When people don't make their intentions clear, it can result in extra costs or, worse, the project being lost. Examples of project specifics include timetables, design, terminology, contracts, price, client instructions, etc. Accountability is key to clarifying. The team will work more productively and with better trust if everyone's duties and expectations are made clear. At work, get into the habit of clarifying and urge your coworkers to do the same. Because unresolved questions impede progress, ask, confirm, and explain.

Overview of the many Communication Styles

Outbound

As for outbound communication styles, the well-known four are forceful, aggressive, passive-aggressive, and passive. But this doesn't really help you get better at communicating with other people, does it? You are truly interested in learning what works best for them.

Inbound

The four primary categories of the DiSC communication model—dominant, influencer, steady, or conscientious—categorize the important inbound communication styles. There will be some overlap; not everyone will fit neatly into one category or the other. But as a general guideline, it's a good place to start.

How to Interact with Dominant Individuals

Dominant folks like having productive, comprehensive talks. Anyone in command of a team or at the top of the professional ladder, including project managers, directors, and CEOs, are frequently dominants. They respond well to a challenge and are goal-oriented, energetic, and action-oriented.

When speaking to them, be as direct as you can. Get to the point quickly and stick to your theme.

Before you speak to them, get ready. Be prepared to respond to inquiries immediately since they prefer to have a plan of action.

Don't take offense if they give you direct responses or appear a bit irritated. They simply want to act as soon as possible and want to be upfront; it's not personal.

Avoid wasting their time by making commitments you can't keep. Niceties like weekend plans, rich praises, or excessive apologies are unnecessary. Less talk, more action, if they had a mantra.

How to talk to Influential People

Influencers like interacting with others and are also known as socializers and initiators. They are the talkative ones in your workplace. They will quickly become friends with the new employee, show visitors around, and offer their opinion on the hottest trends. They perform well under pressure, are readily trusted, and are emotionally sincere. However, they frequently lack attention and dedication, therefore it's best to work on smaller tasks with them.

Be approachable, fun, and let your humor through. They take informal chats well. Write a follow-up to chats to support them. They tend to forget things easily, so having written notes to refer to keeps them grounded and focused. Allow them the space to be creative and expressive. They can help your team's culture by being recruited. If they veer off course, be ready to gently guide them.

Take their optimism with a grain of salt. They frequently overestimate their own skills and those of others around them, which, if not checked, can result in disappointment down the line. Avoid talking too seriously, abruptly, or stuffily. Don't anticipate them to pay attention to minute details.

How to Interact with Responsible Individuals

Conscious individuals, usually referred to as "analyzers," frequently move slowly and steadily. They are extremely skilled and detail-oriented. They may not be the chattiest individuals, but you can always depend on them for accuracy and precision.

Give a lot of information up front and provide notes to accompany in-person talks so they may be referred to later. Being unclear or disorganized might annoy conscientious workers, so try to be as comprehensive or orderly as you can. Give them precise instructions and goals so you can let them handle the work on their own. They prefer to put on their headphones and buckle down than to float around the workplace asking questions or participating in protracted brainstorming sessions because they are typically somewhat introverted. Give them the chance to develop new abilities or showcase their existing ones.

Not rushing them. Before making a choice, they will double-check every available facts, and nothing you say or do will convince them to compromise on their devotion to accuracy. Don't disguise comments as criticism since that can make them feel incredibly demotivated. Avoid chatting about unrelated topics before every work-related conversation. This is not to say that you should never do this; it just means that you should watch for signs from them to see whether they're interested in continuing the discussion. Stop it in its tracks and get back to business if they only have monosyllabic responses. Do not misinterpret their calmer manner for lack of interest. They have enthusiasm within, but they prefer not to spend too much time showing it when they might be working instead. Do not confront them with inquiries in person. These dedicated employees appreciate mental clarity and focus. Instead, try sending them an email or a brief message using the team chat app. They'll be really grateful.

How to Interact with Steady People

Steady individuals, usually referred to as "harmonizers," are patient, devoted, and kind. They collaborate effectively with others and excel in jobs that call for a lot of empathy and assistance. They are fast to fit in and would rather blend in than cause a stir.

Be prepared for them to inquire more and request additional information. Be affable and at ease. Encourage them by complimenting their recent accomplishments, and feel free to talk with them about your weekend before getting down to business. Engage in active listening, and after they speak, follow up with pertinent questions to get them to open up.

Not rushing them. They are inherently risk-averse and enjoy direction and concentration, much like contentious types. Simply because they haven't expressed any disagreement doesn't mean they agree with your proposal. Instead, try asking them directly, particularly in a one-on-one setting so they can consider how to best respond without feeling pressed for time.

Making the Change

It's a good idea to consider your own coworkers now that you are aware of all the major communication types and what approaches are most effective for each of them. You'll be able to interact with them more effectively in the future if you can categorize them as belonging to one or more of these communication styles.

After determining where each individual fits, spend some time analyzing some of your discussions with them. Was there ever a time when you could have spoken to them more effectively? Did they take any action that would make their communication style obvious? You may start to come up with some ideas for how you might enhance communication with them once you have given everything some thought.

Try incorporating these suggestions into your discussion the next time you speak with them, whether the topic is the upcoming project or simply how their weekend went. You'll probably start to notice that your working connection is flourishing more than ever!

 We all have to interact with all sorts of individuals. Wouldn't it be good if we all perceived this disparity as an opportunity rather than a difficulty, rather than avoiding the task?

Working with individuals you instantly click with is excellent, but talking well with someone you wouldn't typically click with may also be quite rewarding. Being a social chameleon Adjust your communication style to that of your coworkers and observe how the dialogues (and productivity) grow.

Conclusion

The ability to communicate effectively is one of the most important skills you can learn. Yet effective communication isn't the only thing that's needed. Dealing with people who have different personalities is what happens; neither you nor they are at fault. But, there are drawbacks. When two people are having trouble talking, a terrible thing typically happens: They start guessing. Nobody likes being misunderstood, and those who have previously had problems coordinating their communication styles will steer clear of future collaboration. If we are conscious of our diverse communication styles, we may be able to achieve more and do so with less anxiety and stress. And that can only be advantageous for teamwork.

Those who are conscious, sometimes referred to as "analyzers," generally walk steadily and slowly. They are incredibly knowledgeable and meticulous. Although they may not be the chattiest people, you can always rely on them for precision and accuracy. Be ready for them to ask more questions and make requests for more details. Chameleon to improve conversations and efficiency, adapt your communication style to that of your coworkers.

Chapter

17

Continuous Learning

Learning never ends because people are always picking up information from their everyday encounters with numerous phenomena in their environment.

The constant extension of knowledge and skill sets is known as continuous learning. Continuous learning in the workplace, which is frequently employed in the context of professional growth, is about acquiring new skills and information while simultaneously consolidating what has already been gained.

The basis for ongoing learning is laid forth by daily routines and activities. Any continual method of knowledge consumption may be used to further learning. It might occur during a certain amount of time or go on for the rest of your life. Continuous learning can be formal, informal, and systematic; the term is wide. Studying, having a casual discussion, practicing the usage of a skill, asking for help with a new subject, observing experienced workers, discovering new and alternative work practices, and attending formal courses are all examples of activities. Employee engagement, job happiness, and knowledge retention have all been found to increase with the use of continuous learning strategies in the workplace. Organizations must continuously adapt to the rapidly shifting social and economic surroundings if they want to remain competitive. Employee skill sets must develop to match the needs of the business environment since the success of an organization depends on the performance of its employees.

Components of Lifelong Learning

The goal of continuous learning in the workplace is for people to maintain their knowledge and abilities throughout time.

According to conventional training methods, an acute training event often results in a peak in employee knowledge, which then steadily declines over time due to a lack of reinforcement.

Employee knowledge is the outcome of several learning experiences in continuous learning. An organization may increase employee knowledge levels through continuous learning, which also sustains the peak with regular practice sessions.

Advantages of Lifelong Learning

In the workplace, ongoing learning has the ability to broaden employee skill sets, improve skill and knowledge retention, spark fresh insights and viewpoints, elevate morale, and improve overall employee performance.

According on the degree of each employee, this can:

- Assist in achieving professional development objectives
- The acquisition or renewal of professional licenses or certificates
- Consider several angles while tackling your job.
- Keep up a professional skill set that is in demand.

Continuous learning has several benefits for the company.

- Support organizational objectives.

- Participate in fostering a culture of innovation that is forward-looking at work

- Make workers feel appreciated by implementing changes that show you care about their personal growth.

- Reduce expenses by investing in the continued education of current employees rather than beginning the training process for a new hire.

Modeling

The continuous learning model by Bersin by Deloitte is structured to measure two scales of tiers in relation to each of its two main considerations:

1. **The purpose of learning is to meet the requirements of the learner:**

- Immediate. What is required now to succeed?

- Intermediate. What is required to develop in present roles and broaden skill sets?

- Transitional. What is required in order to achieve long-term organizational goals, climb the professional ladder, or change careers?

2. **The many settings in which workers learn are known as paradigms. They are made up of "the four E's:**

- Education. Traditional ideas about learning and growth. Usually trackable, with a beginning and a finish that are distinct.

- Experience. This is often learnt through professional activities including stretch assignments, special projects, and job rotations.

- Exposure. What is discovered via encounters and social ties?

- Environment. Infrastructures that facilitate workplace learning for employees.

Ongoing Learning Techniques

Application of continuous learning strategies include:

1. **Structured education. Formal education techniques that are prearranged for particular objectives:**

- Academic programs
- Online education programs
- Workshops/seminars
- Conferences

- Managerial training employee training

1. **Social education. The methods through which humans learn by engaging with and watching others. It can be done in person or online, formally or informally.**

- Discussion/conversation
- Co-working
- collaborating to solve problems
- Coaching/mentoring
- on-the-job instruction

2. **Self-motivated education. Independently conducted tests to increase knowledge and skills it could happen randomly or adhere to a set timetable.**

- Reading and researching
- Exploration and experimentation
- Practice exams

What steps to take?

Organizations must provide a welcoming learning environment if they want to motivate staff to engage in continuous learning. Because they may be preoccupied with using their time to achieve important deadlines, employees could be reluctant to engage in new continuous learning initiatives.

Start by making a plan. Outline a plan of action for workers to see and demonstrate the organization's commitment to ongoing learning. Where learning plans are implemented, such as at the level of the individual employee, team, department, or organization, should be included. To explain goals and priorities, management and workers should have a conversation.

It is crucial for management to clearly demonstrate their complete support for ongoing learning initiatives since culture is something that begins at the top and filters down. Both provide and keep. Maintain a continual learning culture by allocating the right resources to encourage staff learning.

Conclusion

Continuous learning is the process of continually expanding one's knowledge and skill sets. Daily habits and activities lay the groundwork for lifelong learning. As an organization's success depends on the performance of its people, employee skill sets must evolve to meet the demands of the business environment. A peak in employee knowledge is frequently achieved by an acute training event, but according to traditional training techniques, this peak gradually falls over time owing to a lack of reinforcement. Continuous learning may widen employee skill sets, enhance skill and knowledge retention, inspire new ideas and perspectives, boost morale, and enhance overall employee performance in the workplace.

The techniques used by people to learn through interacting with and observing others. Formally or informally, it can be carried out in person or online. Tests that are independently done to improve knowledge and abilities may occur at random or follow a predetermined schedule.

Chapter
18

Success Criteria

Recall that success isn't determined by outcomes but rather by the effort put in to acquire them.

This book aims to show how important it is to establish your own definition of success. I'll be quite direct in my writing.

I'll be direct and I won't pretend that achieving your goals and ambitions will be simple. I want to show that success should only ever be what you define it to be. Success isn't merely measured in dollars and cents. It is not merited by other people's approval.

You have the option of choosing success and a happy life. You can use my definition of success, which I'll provide you later in this book, as a guide, but please only use it that way. I'm hoping you'll take some time to consider what in this life will make you happy, content, and fulfilled.

Coach John Wooden, one of life's great role models, stated that success is "peace of mind," which comes from knowing that you put in the effort to become the greatest version of yourself that you are capable of.

Success is a state of mind. Maximum effort is required for success. It is a state of mind and mental tranquility. Also, pay attention to how much "self" is stressed in self-satisfaction. Never let other people's accolades or approval decide your level of achievement. If that's the case, your life will be quite dismal.

In the past, I would often enter life's situations without giving them much attention. Now, I always ask myself, "What will success look like?" before starting any new projects, businesses, or aspirations in my life.

I've made it a requirement of myself to respond to this issue in light of the strategic course that my career is pursuing. I'm hoping you will, too.

This is quite straightforward, if you have the desire to start anything, you need at the very least have a HUGE vision of your achievement or sense of fulfillment in mind. That is accomplished by using imagination's strength. Organized planning must follow from creative thinking.

The concept of success then comes into play, followed by the objectives, aims, and tasks—from the major to little undertakings. If you're committed to excelling at what you do and realizing your full potential, you'll make the time to decide what success looks like to you.

As I've mentioned in earlier, putting your strategy in book has a special power. Your strategy is visible to you. It's crucial to visualize! Visualization increases your motivation and appetite for reaching your objective. As they light the fire within of you that feeds your ambition and resolve, visualization and imagination go hand in hand.

Speaking your goal and your dreams out has a powerful effect. Last but not least, you combine your written and spoken words with your faith to bind them together; the rest is just a matter of carrying out your plan. As long as you are confident that you are on the correct track, you must have the strength and bravery to move on without stopping.

I want to explain to you why I do what I do and what success means to me personally. I gave each of these a lot of thought, prayer, and self-examination before deciding on them. I urge you to do the same action. My self-assurance has grown significantly. By letting concern and anxiety go, I think I'm moving in the right way.

The benefit of having a plan or road map is that. You might need to sometimes veer off course during rush hour traffic, but your goal is still the same. If we are certain of our destination, navigating the necessary diversions and deviations will be simpler.

I want you to share what success means to you with others and to put it in book. This will breathe life into it! Your success should always be based on the ideals and beliefs you uphold: traits that have endured the test of time and are tried and true.

Characteristics that you have seen and appreciated in the lives of others, whether via contemporary people or historical figures. Characteristics that you already exhibit in your own life and which have aided in your growth in favor, wealth of faith, happiness, and peace of mind.

Live audaciously going forward. You should never accept anything less than what you consider to be your finest.

Conclusion

I'm trying to demonstrate that success should only ever be what you make it. Money isn't the only metric used to determine success. The endorsement of others is not warranted. Success is a mentality. The best effort is necessary for success. It is a mental attitude and calmness. See how strongly the word "self" is emphasized in self-satisfaction as well. It is simple to understand that if you are motivated to start something, you must at the very least have a big picture of your success or sense of fulfillment in mind. It has a significant impact to speak your desire and your objective out. Your objective remains the same, even if you occasionally need to deviate from it due to traffic during rush hour.

The End

Previous Books

Calligraphy

Aljazam Arabic Calligraphy: Beginners Level Sulus Edition (Aljazam Arabic Calligraphy Series Book 1)

History

Time of Babylon: The Throne Series

Time of Egypt: The Throne Series

Time of Persia: The Throne Series

Time of Greece: The Throne Series

Time of China: The Throne Series

Time of Rome: The Throne Series

Technology

Fundamentals of AWS, GCP and Azure Cloud Technology